Contents

Life on eight legs

The world's biggest spider is the South American tarantula, with a 75-millimetre-long body and legs spanning 255 millimetres.

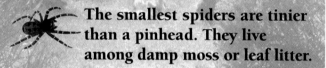
The smallest spiders are tinier than a pinhead. They live among damp moss or leaf litter.

Many spiders live for only one to two years, but tarantulas can live for as long as twenty years!

An extreme fear of spiders is called arachnophobia.

Spiders are generally helpful to humans because they eat insect pests. Only a few species are poisonous to people.

Many spiders do not have a common name. They only have the Latin name given to them by scientists. This is written in *italic letters* in this book.

Spiders belong to the group of animals called the **arachnids**. This group also includes scorpions, harvestmen, mites and ticks. The arachnids are part of a larger group of animals called the **arthropods**. All arthropods have jointed legs and a tough outer layer called the **cuticle** or exoskeleton. This does not stretch, so in order to grow, an arthropod has to shed its skin from time to time. This process is called **moulting**.

spinnerets
Tiny parts from which silk threads are drawn.

abdomen
Rear part of body.

Insects, centipedes and crabs, as well as arachnids, are arthropods. Arachnids are arthropods that have eight legs.

It is easy to tell the difference between spiders and insects – insects have only six legs, and usually have wings. Spiders never have wings.

A spider's body has two sections, connected by a narrow waist. The head and **thorax**, to which all the legs are attached, are joined together to make up the front section, called the **cephalothorax**. The eyes, jaws and mouth, together with a pair of short feeler-like **palps**, are at the front of the head. The back part of the spider is called the **abdomen**. The abdomen contains the gut, **reproductive** and other organs, and the **silk glands**. At its tip are **spinnerets** from which silk is drawn wherever the spider goes. A spider has no bones. Its whole body is supported by a tough outer layer – the **cuticle**.

eyes
Most spiders have eight eyes, but some have six and a few have four or only two eyes.

legs
Each of the eight, jointed legs is made up of seven parts.

mouth
Used for sucking up food. Cannot be seen from above.

fangs
Sharply pointed to pierce body of **prey** and inject **venom**.

palps
Used for feeling and tasting.

cephalothorax
The front part of the body.

jaws
These jaws strike sideways. Some **species** have downward-striking jaws.

claws
Tiny hooks used to walk across **web** and to arrange silk threads.

A common spider, for example a house spider, is patchy-brown in colour, with long legs and a plump abdomen covered with hairs.

Almost all spiders have **venom**-injecting bites, so they can kill their **prey**. Many people are afraid of spiders, but there is really no need to fear most of them. The fangs of most spiders are too small and weak to break our skin. Of those spiders with fangs that can, only a few kinds have venom that is strong enough to be dangerous to humans.

Spiders can thrive wherever there are insects for them to eat. Spiders live in almost all parts of the world, except in the sea, in frozen Antarctica and on the highest mountain tops. A few live within the Arctic Circle, and some spiders live as far south as the islands of South Georgia, near Antarctica. There are spiders in

The female black widow spider has venom that is powerful enough to kill an adult human. She is easily recognized by the red 'hourglass' marking on the underside of her **abdomen**.

deserts, tropical jungles, rainforests, meadows, woodlands and caves. There are even spiders that live in or on lakes and ponds and, as we all know, many spiders live inside our houses.

SPIDER JAWS

The jaws of a tarantula strike downwards, so that the fangs stab into the victim.

The jaws of a wolf spider strike sideways.

DIFFERENT KINDS OF SPIDER

There are over 30,000 different **species**, or kinds, of spider. These are divided into two main groups:
• spiders with jaws that strike downwards
• spiders with jaws that strike sideways.
Tarantulas (sometimes called bird-eating spiders), trapdoor spiders and funnel-**web** spiders belong to the first group.

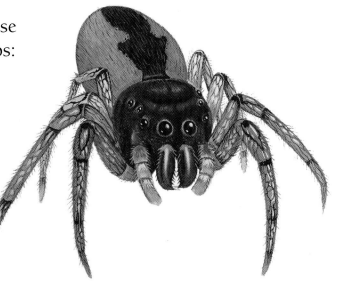

There are at least 2000 different species of jumping spider.

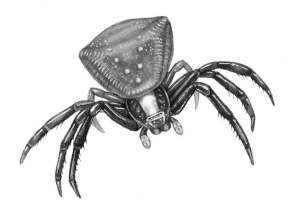

Some spiders, such as crab spiders, are brightly coloured to match the petals of a flower, so that insects cannot see them.

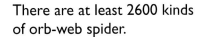

There are at least 2600 kinds of orb-web spider.

All other spiders have jaws that strike sideways. Over 90 families belong to this second group, including wolf spiders, jumping spiders, comb-footed spiders, recluse spiders, orb-web spiders, money spiders, crab spiders – and many others!

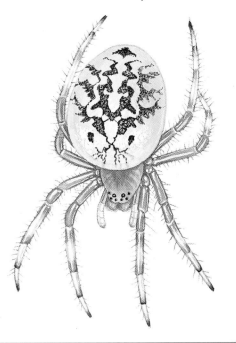

EYES

Most spiders have eight tiny eyes – two 'main eyes' and six 'secondary eyes'. The rest have six, four or two eyes. Although this seems like a lot of eyes, in fact a spider's eyesight is usually not very good. Many **species** can tell only whether it is light or dark. Jumping and wolf spiders are exceptions. Their main eyes face forwards and can focus on objects up to 18 centimetres away. The secondary eyes are on the sides of the head. These give the spiders a good view and enable them to judge distances.

Six of a wolf spider's eyes face forwards, and two are on the top of the head. These can see out to the sides and a short distance behind the spider.

GOOD VIBRATIONS

Spiders do not have ears, but they are very sensitive to **vibrations**. These are picked up with special hairs on the spider's legs. The hairs are connected to nerves that carry messages to its brain. A few, such as the male buzzing spider, make vibrations that people can hear. These are made to attract females. As well as being able to pick up vibrations, the legs and **palps** of a spider help it to taste its food and work out where it is.

Sharing your home

Houses attract flies, mosquitoes and other kinds of insects, so it is not surprising that spiders also move in. Daddy-long-legs spiders make untidy **webs** up near the ceiling and under shelves.

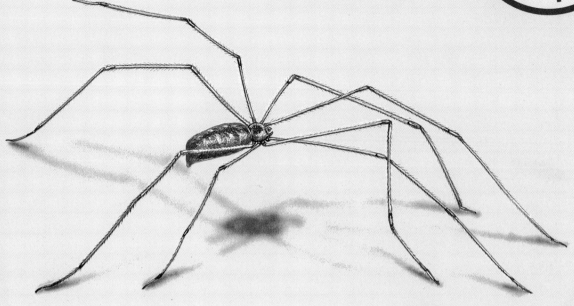

House spiders live lower down, behind cupboards, in garages, sheds and other dark places. This is the spider that causes alarm when it climbs into the bath overnight and cannot get out!

Spider silk

A spider's silk is very useful. It can be used to trap **prey** and to stop it from escaping, to line burrows (see page 21) and to make a shelter under a leaf. A female spider uses her silk to wrap up her eggs; a male spider uses silk during **mating**. All spiders leave a line of silk, called a **dragline**, wherever they go. This means that if they jump from a twig to escape sudden danger, or they are knocked from their perch by a passing animal, they can get safely back home by climbing up the dragline.

Silk is produced in **glands** inside a spider's **abdomen**. It is made up of a **protein** called **fibroin**. Inside the

 The silk that a golden orb-web spider uses to make its dragline is the strongest natural fibre.

 The diameter of spider silk is about three thousandths of a millimetre.

 A golden orb-web spider can produce a single line of silk 700 metres long.

 Comb-footed and orb-web spiders make sticky silk for parts of their webs.

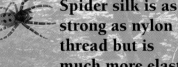 Spider silk is as strong as nylon thread but is much more elastic.

 It would take 27,648 female garden spiders to make half a kilogram of silk.

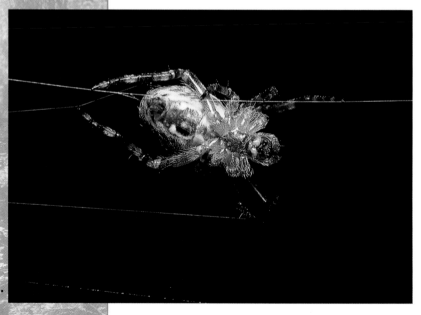

This female orb-web spider is using her feet to hold the strands of silk and attach them in exactly the right place to start her web.

silk glands, fibroin is liquid. It trickles down the

finger-like **spinnerets** and is pulled out by the spider's feet. As it is pulled, the liquid silk becomes solid strands. The spider uses its feet to make it into sheets, **webs** or egg sacs.

SPINNERETS

A spider has tiny, finger-like parts called spinnerets at the tip of its abdomen. Silk is drawn out of the spinnerets through tiny holes. Most kinds of spiders have three pairs of spinnerets. The rest have two pairs. The third pair has become a pair of flat plates that

No matter how far the spider falls, it will be able to return to its perch by climbing up its silk dragline.

have as many as 40,000 even smaller holes. The silk that is pulled through these is the finest of all spider silk. It is called 'hackled' band silk. It is not sticky, but because it is so fine, it instantly clings to an insect's legs and body.

A drop of liquid silk trickles from each tiny hole in the spider's spinnerets. It pulls each of these into a fine silk thread.

13

NIMBLE FOOTWORK

As a spider spins its silk into a **web**, or wraps up an insect it has caught, it controls the silk threads with tiny hooks on each foot. With these, it can arrange each thread in exactly the right place. It can also move about over its own silk threads without getting tangled.

Spiders that do not make webs have two tiny hooks on their feet, but web builders have three. The third hook presses the silk strands against **barbed hairs**, enabling the spider to build its complicated webs. Tufts of hairs on some spiders' feet also help them to cling to upright or very smooth surfaces without falling.

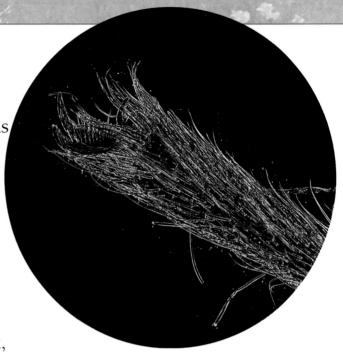

The feet of this web-building spider have three hooks. The third hook holds the silk by pressing it against tufts of hairs.

BALLOONING

If you look up into the air on a warm summer's afternoon, the chances are that you will see the

Very small spiders and spiderlings release long lines of silk that are pulled by breezes. The tiny spiders can then drift for long distances, spreading out to find new places to live.

sunlight shine on drifting lengths of spider silk. Or you may be surprised when a sheet-web spider lands on your arm, and seems to come out of nowhere. In fact, the sheet-web spider has been drifting in the air on the end of a stretch of its silk. This is known as **ballooning**. Young **spiderlings** of many kinds 'balloon' in order to move about, but adult sheet-web spiders are still small enough to 'balloon' from place to place.

I DIDN'T KNOW THAT

Underwater spider

The European water spider actually lives underwater, but it still needs to breathe and feed in air. It spins a silk sheet among water plants and carries air bubbles from the surface that it stores beneath the sheet to make an air-filled dome. Air is carried between the spider's back legs and **abdomen**. The spider lives in its air-filled tent, only leaving to catch **prey** or bring more air down from above.

Wonderful webs

 It takes a garden spider about one hour to make a web.

 Tropical golden orb-web spiders make webs almost 2 metres across with silk so strong it catches bats and small birds.

 The biggest webs of all are built by social spiders that live together in large colonies. They join webs to make one enormous web.

 A colony of Panamanian social spiders may have as many as 10,000 spiders!

 A bolas spider puts a blob of sticky silk on the end of a line of silk and swings this to catch flying moths.

A spider's **web** is a clever trap for catching insects and other small animals. Different kinds of spiders build very different kinds of webs. The simplest web of all is no more than silk trip-lines stretching out from the entrance of a silk tube. Other spiders make much more complicated webs. Some look like sheets of silk, and others are three-dimensional tangles of threads. Most amazing of all are the beautifully made orb webs hung in just the right place to catch flying insects. When a spider has made its web, all it has to do is wait patiently for its **prey** to stumble into it. When this happens, the captive's struggles alert the spider to dart out and grab it.

Sticky silk has droplets of gluey liquid strung out all along it.

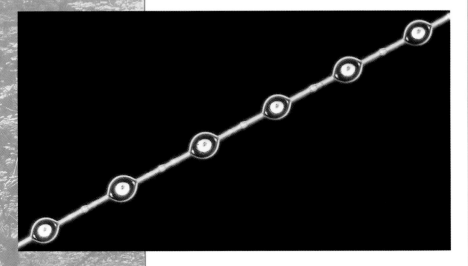

Lace-web spiders and garden spiders have extra tricks to make their webs even better at catching their next meal. Lace-web spiders make parts of their webs with extremely fine 'hackled' band silk. The hairs and hooks on an insect's feet get really tangled up in this. Garden spiders make the 'spokes' of their orb webs of dry silk, but the spiral threads are made of sticky silk. Sticky silk comes from

Dewdrops clinging to the silk of this garden spider's web show up the spokes and spiral threads of this insect-catching net.

special **silk glands**. As the spider weaves it into a web, it plucks each thread, causing the sticky coating to separate into droplets. An insect's feet get stuck in this, but the spider does not. The spider walks only on the dry, non-sticky silk of the spokes.

17

SCAFFOLD WEBS

Comb-footed spiders build 'scaffold **webs**'. These untidy webs are made of a central tangle of threads that is attached to nearby plant stems by other tightly stretched threads. The threads are strung with gluey droplets, a bit like tiny beads.

Untidy scaffold webs are a mass of sticky threads stretching across twigs and leaves to trap the small flying insects that also live or feed there.

When an insect stumbles into the tightly stretched threads, they break and pull tight, carrying the insect into the middle of the sticky web.

Sheet-web weavers dart out from their hiding place the instant they sense anything twitching the silk threads of their 'sheet'.

SHEETS AND HAMMOCKS

Sheet-web spiders make webs that look just like sheets of silk covering the ground or plants. At one end of the sheet, the spider makes a tunnel of silk, tucked under a rock or between plant stems, where it waits for something to land on its web.

Dwarf spiders also make sheets of web, but these are found higher up among plant stems or grasses. The sheet is more like a hammock, with strands of silk stretching from the top of the sheet and into the nearby plants. An insect flying into these upper threads falls on to the hammock and is caught by the spider.

Sheet-web spiders are common in grassy places, where they spin their small hammock-like webs between the grass stems. The spider bites its **prey** from below and drags it through the web.

Throwing a net

Ogre-faced spiders spin a little web of stretchy silk that they hold out between their front three pairs of legs. The back legs hold on to a strand of silk so that the spider is hanging upside down, just a few centimetres above the ground. When an insect walks or flies below the spider, it drops the net over it.

ORB WEBS

An orb **web** is an almost circular net. Spiders choose gaps between plant stems or corners of buildings to make these webs. They have a framework of threads that point outwards like the spokes of a bicycle wheel. These are joined by spiral threads to make the net. The way in which an orb-web spider builds its web is fascinating (see diagram below). First, the spider pulls a thread of silk that is carried in the air until it touches a nearby stem. The spider makes this stronger with a line of silk. From this line, the spider makes a Y-shape. The point where all three parts of the 'Y' meet becomes the centre of the new web. More and more lines are made between the centre and outer frame. The spider then spins the spiral. In the centre of the web, where the spider often waits for a catch, the spiral is made of dry silk. The rest is spun with thread coated with sticky droplets.

PURSE WEBS

Instead of spinning a web that traps insects that stumble into it, the purse-web spider makes a silk tube, or purse, that lies on the surface of the ground. To hide it, the spider covers the 'purse' with pieces of dead leaves or twigs. The open end of the purse leads into a

HOW AN ORB-WEB SPIDER SPINS ITS WEB

1. The spider pulls a thread of silk and lets the breeze carry it to a twig. It then runs along this thread, making it stronger with more silk.

2. The spider makes a Y-shaped framework below the first thread, and attaches it to a lower twig.

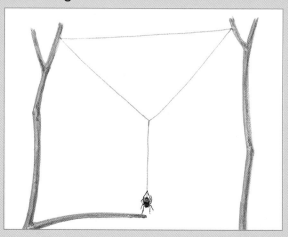

silk-lined, underground burrow. The spider waits inside until an insect walks over the purse. Then it stabs its **prey** through the silk wall of the purse and drags it into the burrow.

1. An insect walks over the dry leaves that hide the purse web.

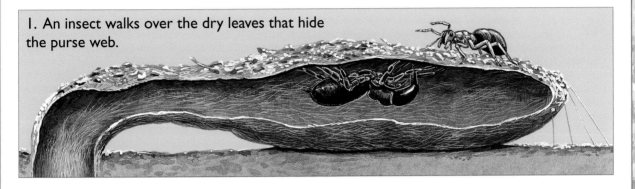

2. The purse-web spider bites its prey through the web, and pulls it inside.

3. Then the spider makes an outer frame, and starts to spin lines from the centre of the web to the frame.

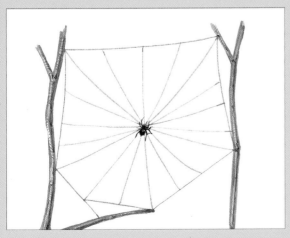

4. The spider spins a strengthening spiral, and finally, a spiral of sticky threads that will catch its prey.

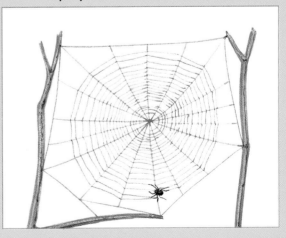

Hunters

All spiders are **predators** that need to catch live **prey**, but only some of them are active hunters. If you watch a brick or stone wall on a sunny day, the dull brown or blackish spiders that you see running over it in short, fast sprints are mostly wolf spiders. They have good eyesight and are on the look-out for movements that may mean a good meal is close by. A catch is made after some creeping and sprinting, with a final pounce on to their prey. As you are watching wolf spiders, you might find that a jumping spider or a lynx spider is watching you!

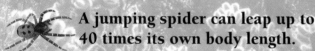

A jumping spider can leap up to 40 times its own body length.

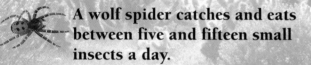

A wolf spider catches and eats between five and fifteen small insects a day.

A little jumping spider eats about six insects a day, including plant-eating leaf-hoppers.

Spiders that hunt at night have poor eyesight and rely on other senses to find and catch their prey. They live under wood, leaf litter, or in holes in buildings. They find slow-moving insects and other **invertebrates** by feeling around with their front legs.

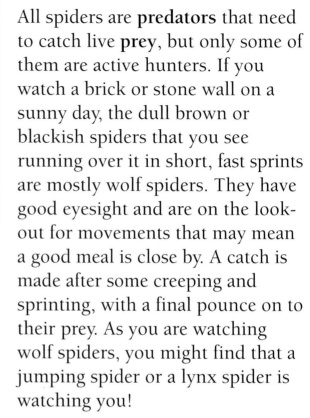

Wolf spiders, like this one from Arizona, USA, can run quickly over the ground both to catch prey and to escape from danger.

JUMPING SPIDERS

Unlike the mostly dull-coloured wolf spiders, jumping spiders are often brightly patterned. Although they are rather small spiders, their two main eyes are large and easy to see. Attracted by a moving insect, and able to see clearly how far away it is, these spiders catch their prey by leaping on it from quite a long distance. Some can even make **vertical** leaps of up to 15 centimetres. Their silk **dragline** stops them from falling to the ground. They just run back up the line with their catch.

A jumping spider pushes off with its back legs and sails through the air. As it jumps, a dragline of silk is pulled from its **spinnerets**.

STICKY SPIT

Spitting spiders have an unusual way of catching their prey. They are small spiders that have quite poor eyesight. When a fly lands near by, or the spider manages to creep up close, it traps its prey by spitting a jet of sticky liquid from each jaw. By quickly moving its head from side to side as it is spitting, the spider pins down the insect with two zigzags of gum. Then the spitting spider can kill and eat its prey.

The woodlouse spider likes to stay hidden, but be warned – if you pick one up, its powerful fangs give a painful bite.

jump out at visiting insects. Often they choose a flower that matches their colour, but sometimes they get it wrong and sit on petals of the wrong shade. They are able to change colour slightly over a few days to get a better match.

SLOW BUT TOUGH

Slow-moving woodlice rely on a hard outer layer like armour to keep them safe. The woodlouse spider specializes in catching and eating these **crustaceans**. It catches woodlice by piercing their armour with very hard, sharp **fangs**. It twists sideways to bite the woodlouse so that one fang pierces the softer underside, and the other fang stabs through the upper side.

LYING IN WAIT

Female crab spiders have plump bodies that are white, greenish, yellow or even pink. They sit in flowers waiting to

Perfectly matched with the yellow buttercup, this crab spider is ready to catch any other insect that visits this flower.

Tiny thieves

Tiny *Argyrodes* spiders live on the **webs** of other kinds of spiders and feed on insects that are caught in their webs. The true owner of the web is often a much larger spider and may not bother to eat the small insects that get caught in its web, so the 'thief' keeps the web tidy. However, these tiny spiders also feed on the owner's **prey** and sometimes kill and eat the owner!

After the catch

Timid black widow spider females have venom about fifteen times more powerful than rattlesnake venom, but the amount injected is far smaller. It can cause death in humans, but there is now a medicine to stop its harmful effects.

The Australian Sydney funnel-web spider will attack anything close to it that moves, and its fangs can even go through fingernails. Bites have caused death in as little as fifteen minutes.

The aggressive Brazilian wandering spider, with a 13-centimetre legspan and the biggest venom glands of all spiders, will run at people to bite them.

Bites from recluse spiders are slow to heal and can cause death. They are not aggressive and are often found in houses in the USA.

When an insect is caught in a **web**, it struggles to escape. If it is really lucky, it manages to tear a large hole in the web and breaks free. Most captives are not this lucky. Within about five seconds, the spider has run from its lair and bitten them. Many insects could sting or bite the spider. To stop this, a spider has to attack its **prey** quickly. Each bite injects drops of **venom** that quickly **paralyse** or kill the insect.

This spider is taking no chances. While its venom is working, the butterfly is wrapped in a wide band of silk so that it cannot struggle free.

The venom is made in **glands** at the base of each jaw. When the spider bites, muscles move and squeeze the glands, so that venom trickles down canals inside each **fang** and out through small holes at the tip. The sharply pointed fangs break weak spots in an insect's tough, outer coat, and the venom works quickly. A spider may wait until it has killed the insect, but orb-web spiders and some others start to wrap their catch in bands of silk straight away.

Bites from some spiders can kill humans. A few, such as the Brazilian wandering spider and the Sydney funnel-web spider, are aggressive and will try to bite anyone that comes near. Others, even some of the most dangerous kinds, are really quite **timid**. Black widow and recluse spiders (neither of which are found in northern Europe) only bite people if they feel threatened. Unfortunately, accidents happen when these spiders enter houses and hide in beds or clothing. They may not be seen by someone climbing into bed or pulling on a sweatshirt.

This highly venomous Sydney funnel-web spider is in a common threat position. It has raised its front legs and its **palps**, and a drop of venom glistens on the tip of each fang.

When they are pressed between cloth and skin, black widow spiders and recluse spiders bite to protect themselves.

It is important for anyone who has been bitten by a dangerously **venomous** spider to get medical help quickly. However, it is also important to remember that most kinds of spiders are harmless. Only about 500 of the thousands and thousands of different **species** have **fangs** that are strong enough to break human skin, and of these, less than 30 have venom strong enough to affect a human.

LIQUIDIZERS

Spiders eat only liquid or semi-liquid food. A spider's fangs cannot slice up and chew **prey**, although on the base of each jaw there are sometimes small teeth that can crush prey. When venom is injected, **digestive juices** also enter the body of the prey. These juices get to work on the soft insides of the body, turning them into a mushy soup. The spider sucks up this soup, leaving all the hard parts behind. After a crab spider has fed, just an empty shell is left, but

Wandering spiders search for food during the night, and are large enough to catch and eat big insects such as grasshoppers and even small tree frogs. This species is not dangerous to humans.

spiders that crush their prey while the digestive juices are working leave a shapeless mess.

Food travels down the spider's throat by a sucking action from the stomach. Solid pieces get caught on hairs that grow in the mouth and throat, and are eventually spat out.

VARIED DIET

Most spiders eat insects, and some feed on other small **invertebrates**. Those that spin **webs** catch flying insects and crawling kinds that accidentally fall into their webs. The spider will not eat everything that becomes tangled in its web though. A small spider may cut the silk around a stinging bee or wasp so that it falls from the web. Some insects make horrible smells or spray out nasty liquids to put off **predators** such as spiders. These are also set free.

Trapdoor spiders lie in wait for prey inside their burrow. They dart out and snatch anything that walks past their trapdoor. Once they have taken their prey inside, they decide whether it is good to eat or not. Grasshoppers, beetles, or shieldbugs that make horrible smells are quickly thrown out of the burrow.

Snake eaters

I DIDN'T KNOW THAT

Large tarantulas may sometimes eat birds, but they mostly eat frogs, lizards and small snakes. In **captivity**, a *Grammostola* spider killed and ate a venomous rattlesnake that was 46 centimetres long! Mice and young rats are also eaten if the spider can catch them.

Reproduction

Male and female spiders must get together to **mate**. Only then can a female lay the eggs that will hatch into the next generation of spiders. A male spider has to approach a female carefully. He is usually much smaller than she is and does not want to be mistaken for **prey**. A female spider is bigger than her mate because her body has to contain the eggs until they are ready to be laid. Some female spiders do indeed eat their mates, but, as males usually die shortly after mating, this means that their bodies are not wasted.

A male golden orb-web spider is so much smaller than the female that he is not worth eating. He is at no risk as he crosses her web and mates with her.

 A large female tarantula lays up to 3000 eggs in one clutch.

 The tiny *Oonops* spider lays just two eggs at a time.

 A female golden orb-web spider may weigh 100 times more than her mate.

 Male grass spiders hold the jaws of their mate open so that the females cannot bite them.

The male crab spider spins silk around the female while they mate.

The **nutrients** from the eaten male help to produce a large **clutch** of eggs. Even if they do not get eaten by their hungry mates, male spiders play no part in caring for their young.

Male spiders use several ways to announce their arrival. If they are accepted, they come closer and stroke the female with their front legs. This calms her, so that mating can take place. After mating, a lucky male leaves and may start looking for another female. Inside the female, the eggs start to develop.

This male garden spider (left) is in danger of being eaten by his fat-bodied mate. He signals to her by vibrating his legs and plucking her web.

SIGNALS

Male jumping spiders and wolf spiders signal to their long-sighted females by waving their front legs or **palps**. Sometimes they add to these signals with side to side movements or leg **vibrations**. *Zygiella* spiders vibrate the female's **web** to signal to each other. First the male plucks a strand of the female's web. Then she answers, also by plucking strands of her web.

Egg laying

Before laying her eggs, a female spider spins a small sheet of silk. This may be flat or cup-shaped. When it is ready, she lays her **clutch** of eggs on the silk sheet. The eggs and the sheet on which they were laid are now closed up in more silk to make an **egg sac**. A daddy-long-legs spider makes a flimsy egg sac that she holds in her jaws until the **spiderlings** hatch.

This spider makes her egg sac in a curled leaf and then stands over it, but by the time the eggs hatch, she will have died.

Wolf spiders and many other kinds make a much tougher egg sac. Wolf spider mothers carry their sacs around by holding them with their **spinnerets**. Sheet-**web** and lynx spiders are among those that stand guard over their egg sac until the eggs hatch.

Hatching

Inside each egg, a spider starts to develop, fed by the egg yolk. When it is ready to hatch, it tears the eggshell with a tiny egg tooth on its head. When first hatched, a tiny

If anything disturbs these tiny garden spiders, they immediately scatter in all directions. This means that a **predator** will only be able to catch a few of them.

The tiny young spiders usually stay crowded together until after their second moult.

CARING MOTHERS

After they have laid their eggs, some female spiders take no more care of the egg sac at all, but many protect their precious eggs. Lynx, crab spiders and others stand guard over their egg sacs. Wolf and swamp spiders are among those that carry their egg sacs around with them all the time.

The nursery-web spider carries her egg sac gripped in her jaws. She chooses to sit in sunny places to keep it warm and dry.

spiderling is unable to spin silk or catch **prey**. Until its first **moult**, it still feeds on the rest of the yolk, safe inside the egg sac. Within a day or two, it moults and, together with all the other spiderlings, leaves the egg sac.

Pardosa wolf spider mothers still care for their young even after they have hatched. The tiny **spiderlings** climb on to their mother's **abdomen**. She carries around her group of tiny babies until their second **moult**. Then the young spiderlings are ready to take care of themselves.

As her name suggests, a female nursery-web spider spins a tent like a 'nursery' of silk over herself

The abdomen of this female wolf spider is completely hidden by her group of tiny young spiders. If one falls off, it just climbs back up its silk **dragline**.

just before the spiderlings hatch. These tents are made between blades of grass, and the spiderlings stay together inside.

HOW SPIDERS GROW

Young spiders are miniature versions of their parents, but they cannot **mate** and **reproduce** until they are adults. Their tough outer layer, the **cuticle**, is not very stretchy, so spiders have to moult in order to grow. The old skin splits along the sides. The spider wriggles to make the split larger and pulls out its eight legs. The damp, new cuticle is soft and stays

Food sharing

The female comb-footed spider makes a liquid in her mouth that her spiderlings feed on for several days. Then she shares her food with her tiny young. She crushes her **prey** so that her spiderlings can feed on the liquids that ooze out.

stretchy until it dries. A freshly moulted spider is larger than it was before. Skins that have been shed can often be seen hanging in spiders' webs. Once they are adults, most spiders no longer moult, but tarantulas, which live a long time, do keep moulting.

Moulting is a dangerous time for a spider. Even after it has wriggled out of its old skin, it cannot run from danger until its new skin has hardened.

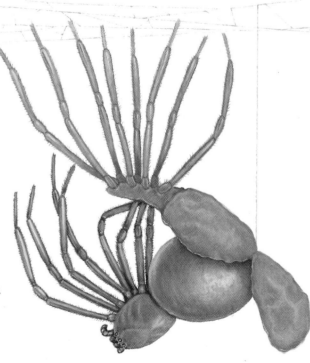

Survival tactics

The world is a dangerous place for spiders, because there are so many larger **predators** eager to eat them. Some **species** simply hide to keep out of harm. Huntsman spiders hide under bark or stones. Some make burrows or spin silk tubes. Trapdoor spiders close their burrows with lids, and a female trapdoor spider spends all her long life inside her burrow. Life is more dangerous for a male trapdoor spider, who has to leave his burrow to find a **mate**.

The California trapdoor spider can hold the lid to its burrow shut even if a force 38 times its own weight is trying to pull it up.

One tropical crab spider looks exactly like a shiny, fresh bird dropping that has just landed on a leaf.

Blending in with a background of bark, leaves or petals is another way of hiding from a predator. This kind of disguise is called **camouflage**. Australian lichen spiders live and hunt on tree trunks covered with flaky patches of lichen. They are camouflaged to look just like the lichen-covered bark. Some crab spiders are the same colour as flower petals. Tropical lynx spiders sit in the middle of leaves, but they are hard to spot because they are bright green, just like the leaf.

A goldenrod spider can change colour to match the flower it is sitting on. It can even turn pink. As long as it keeps still, a sharp-eyed predator will not see it.

birds into thinking that they are something more dangerous, like a stinging wasp.

HIDDEN ENTRANCE

Trapdoor spiders close their burrows with a variety of clever hinged lids. These help to hide the burrows, and so protect the spider. The burrows are sometimes over 30 centimetres deep, and are dug by the spider using its jaws. The spider makes the wall smooth with a mixture of mud and saliva and lines it with silk. The tightly-fitting lids are made of bits of bark, soil, or twigs, bound together with silk.

Another kind of disguise is known as **mimicry**. By looking like another kind of animal altogether, spiders trick predators such as

Pointed parts on the back of this bark spider are a good copy of the spines on the twig. The spider is also the same colour as the twig, which makes it very difficult to see.

37

Some Australian trapdoor spiders have secret side 'trapdoors' or emergency exits from their burrows. The pellet spider is even more clever. As well as a trapdoor at the entrance, this spider digs a shallow hole in the side, halfway down the burrow. It makes a pear-shaped 'pellet' from mud, saliva and silk and places this in the hole. If anything enters its burrow, it pulls on the silk to flip the pellet so that it blocks the lower part of the burrow, in which the spider is hiding.

When a trapdoor spider wants to leave its burrow, it lifts the close-fitting lid and carefully looks out. If it senses danger, it darts back inside, pulling the lid shut.

ARMOUR PLATING

A burrow can become a dangerous place if a spider suddenly finds itself trapped inside. *Cyclocosmia truncata* spiders have a thick, very tough shield on the end of their **abdomens** to keep **predators** from pulling them out of their burrows. This shield can be used to plug the narrow end at the bottom of the burrow.

MASTERS OF MIMICRY

Many birds eat spiders, but fewer eat stinging ants because if there is one ant there are usually hundreds, swarming all over the place. Some jumping spiders are protected from these birds by looking just like ants. They even

Itchy hairs

Tarantulas have very hairy legs and bodies. The hairs are **barbed** and break off easily, so if a spider is attacked by an enemy, it scratches off clouds of these hairs from its back and flicks them into the enemy's face. They stick and make the thin skin of the nose and mouth of predators very itchy. They also affect human skin.

wave their front pair of legs the way an ant waves its antennae (feelers), and run about like ants as well.

A jumping spider from Borneo **mimics** a wasp in an unusual way. The front part of the spider's abdomen looks like the wasp's abdomen, and the rear part looks like the wasp's head. The spider's **spinnerets** mimic wasp feelers and jaws. If a predator attacks the 'false' head, the spider can cause confusion by running 'backwards'.

The abdomen of jumping spiders is shaped to look like a wasp's head and **thorax**. The spider's real head is at the top left in this picture.

Spiders under threat

Even though a female spider may lay hundreds of eggs, few survive long enough to **reproduce**. Spiders face many dangers, even the largest kinds. Some simply die of starvation or lack of water. Many are eaten by birds. Others are eaten by small **mammals**, lizards, frogs, toads or even pet cats. Others face something even more horrible – they are eaten by wasp grubs while they are still alive.

People are also a threat to spiders. Rainforest spiders are under threat because every year more and more

The Mexican red-kneed spider, a kind of tarantula, has become so popular as a pet it is protected under CITES (Convention on International Trade in Endangered Species).

At least 16 kinds of spiders are on the IUCN (International Union for Conservation of Nature and Natural Resources) list of threatened species.

The rarest spider in the UK is the lace-web or carmine jumping spider, last seen in the 1950s. Only seven of these have ever been collected.

Male trapdoor spiders are in greatest danger when they leave the safety of their burrows to search for a female.

Chemicals used to spray these orange trees to kill harmful insects also kill the spiders that would eat these insects.

This spider looks dead, but it is not. It has just been paralysed by the wasp's sting. The spider will be eaten alive by the wasp's grub.

of the forest is cut down by people. Some **species** of large tarantulas have become rare because too many have been collected so that people can keep them as pets.

The use of chemicals on farms and in gardens is another danger. Not only are spiders as well as insect pests killed by these chemicals, but they reduce the number of insects on which any surviving spiders can feed.

WILY WASPS

Spider-hunting wasps fly low over the floors of tropical rainforests looking for tarantulas or the burrows in which they hide. When they find one, they **paralyse** it with a **venomous** sting. If it is not already in a burrow, the wasp drags it to its own burrow. The wasp lays a single egg on the spider's body. When the grub hatches, it feeds on the spider, slowly eating it alive.

SPIDER-EATING BIRDS

Around the world, all sorts of small birds search treetops, bushes, under fallen leaves, in holes of bark, around windows and on lawns in their hunt for spiders, insects and other **invertebrates**. Some specialize in eating spiders. The long-billed spiderhunter is one of ten kinds of spiderhunters from south-east Asia that snatch spiders from their **webs** with their curved beaks, before they can run and hide.

DEADLY DAMSELFLIES

The helicopter damselfly from Central America eats only spiders. These damselflies are very long but extremely thin, and their flimsy wings span 19 centimetres. They have good eyesight. When one spots a spider, it flutters a short distance away without being noticed. Then with a sudden burst of speed, it snatches the spider from its web, bites off the juicy **abdomen**, and lets the legs, head, and jaws fall.

SPRING-CLEANING

The spiders that share our houses with us are in great danger from dusters, vacuum cleaners and other household appliances. Almost all of these spiders do no harm at all to people, and even help to keep down insect invaders. Their webs can attract dust and make an annoying mess though, so out they go!

Stonechats are just one of many kinds of small birds that search trees and bushes for spiders and insects to eat. However well-hidden, if the spider moves, then the bird will spot it.

Sneaky spiders

Many kinds of spiders will eat each other if they get the chance. Pirate spiders specialize in eating comb-footed spiders. These small spiders enter the comb-footed spider's web and pretend to be a struggling insect. When the spider rushes out, it is caught and killed by a very strong bite to one of its front legs. Young spiders may also eat each other if they cannot find other **prey**, and some kinds feed on the body of their dead mother. Perhaps most horrible of all is the habit of many female spiders, like this crab spider, of eating the poor male either before or just after **mating**.

Glossary

abdomen back part of a spider's body, containing the gut, reproductive and other organs and the silk glands

arachnids group of arthropods, all having four pairs of legs

arthropods invertebrate animals that have a tough outer layer called a cuticle, or exoskeleton, and jointed legs

ballooning way in which many small or young spiders float through the air on long threads of silk

barbed hairs hairs which have hooks at the end of them

camouflage colours or patterns that allow an animal to blend in with its background

captivity place that is not an animal's natural home but where it is forced to live

cephalothorax front section of a spider's body, made up of its head and thorax

clutch group of eggs

colony large number of animals of the same species, living closely together

crustacean group of arthropod animals with hard shells, such as crabs, lobsters, shrimps, barnacles and woodlice

cuticle tough outer layer, or exoskeleton, of a spider or insect that supports and protects the body within it

digestive juices fluids that dissolve food in the stomach

dragline line of silk that spiders leave behind them wherever they go. It allows them to drop to the ground safely and to climb back up.

egg sacs silk case in which the mother spider wraps her eggs

fangs long, thin, pointed teeth through which venom is injected

fibroin protein from which spider silk is made

gland organ in an animal's body that produces specific substances

'hackled' band silk finest of all spider silk

invertebrates animals that do not have a backbone

mammal animal with hair or fur, whose young feed on milk produced by their mother

mate (noun) one of a pair of animals that join together to reproduce

mate (verb) joining together of two animals of opposite sexes to reproduce

mimicry protective feature in which one animal looks like another kind of animal or object, allowing it to trick predators into thinking that it is dangerous or not good to eat

moult to shed the whole outer layer of skin

nutrient substance that nourishes or feeds a plant or an animal and helps it to grow

palps pair of short, feeler-like parts on each side of a spider's mouth

paralyse make something unable to move

predator animal that catches and eats other animals

prey animal that is caught and eaten by another animal

protein substance that plays an important role in the bodies of plants and animals

reproduce to produce young

silk glands organs inside the spider's abdomen that produce silk

species kind of animal

spiderling young spider

spinnerets tiny finger-like projections at the tip of the spider's abdomen through which silk is drawn

thorax part of the front section of a spider's body that bears its legs

timid easily frightened

venom poisonous liquid injected into the body of another animal by fangs, claws or stings

vertical upright

vibrate shake or tremble

web silk trap a spider weaves to catch its prey

Further information

Books

Animals Under Logs and Stones, Philip C. Wheater (Richmond Publishing Company, 1996)

Collins Field Guide: Spiders of Britain and Northern Europe, Michael J Roberts (Collins, 1995)

Spiders, Rose Impey (Oxford University Press, 2000)

Websites

http://members.aol.com/YESedu   Go to 'minibeast world: insects and spiders'

http://worldkids.net   Go to 'critters', 'bugs', 'spiders'.

Disclaimer
All the Internet addresses (URLs) given in this book were valid at the time of going to press. However, due to the dynamic nature of the Internet, some addresses may have changed, or sites may have ceased to exist since publication. While the author and publishers regret any inconvenience this may cause readers, no responsibility for any such changes can be accepted by either the author or the publishers.

Index

Numbers in *italic* indicate pictures

contents

so, what is fashion?

In developed societies such as in the western world, many people care about being fashionable. This means they must be seen wearing the latest style of clothing. Also their homes should contain the latest designs in the latest colours – because fashion is not confined to clothes. In fact, fashions affect many areas of life: cars, eating places, furniture, leisure activities, toys, bags and so on.

▲ One of the top designers in haute couture, John Galliano.

Of course, not everyone is interested in keeping pace with the changing face of fashion, and not everyone can afford to, either. However, today's cheaper fabrics and production methods mean that fashionable clothes are more readily available to a wider market. In the past, fashion was exclusive to the upper classes, and everyone else wore whatever clothes they could obtain, usually until the item fell apart. Fashions also changed at a much slower pace, whereas today's 'throw-away' society is prepared to wear items of clothing for a short period of time and then discard them for something new.

Types of fashion

When considering fashion as an idea, people may straightaway think of big-name designers, and catwalks displaying outrageous clothes, but this is just one aspect of fashion. **Couture** fashion is the exclusive and very expensive clothing made by fashion designers for individual **clients**. When a client sees a design they like in the designer's latest collection, they will have the garment or outfit made to order. Designers of couture fashion include John Galliano, Jean-Paul

Gaultier, Christian Lacroix, Karl Lagerfeld, Chanel and Vivienne Westwood.

A less exclusive area of fashion wear is known as designerwear. These are garments that carry a designer label and are sold in shops and stores. They are not as expensive as couture clothes, making them available to a wider market. Names associated with designer wear include Pierre Cardin, Liz Claiborne, Jasper Conran, Donna Karan and Calvin Klein.

Street fashion – the type of garments you see in most high street stores – is affordable fashion for the mass population. It is made possible by the wider range of cheaper fabrics and faster production methods that we have today. It is aimed at young people who want to keep pace with the ever-changing face of fashion. These clothes are not made to last a long time, as the target market is likely to replace their clothes fairly

Designers display their collections on the catwalk to fashion buyers, the fashion press and invited guests. ▶

regularly. This fast turnover in fashion is naturally welcomed and encouraged by the clothing industry. It also fits in with society's ever-increasing desire for consumer spending.

Some styles of clothing are referred to as classic fashions. These are clothes that can be worn for a number of years without looking dated or old fashioned. They tend to be garments without a lot of detail, because detail is often the focus of fashion and it can pigeon-hole a garment into a specific year or season. A simple wool dress or a functional raincoat are examples of classic outfits. These garments are likely to be more expensive than street fashion because they are designed to last for a number of years. They also demand more labour and require higher quality fabrics.

A fad is a very short-lived fashion, lasting for just a few weeks or perhaps a few months. A fad is not likely to be an expensive fashion and may be something as simple as the way to tie (or not tie!) training shoes.

Designer fashion

In the fashion industry, months of hard work for designers culminate in the twice yearly collections. These are more of a fashion extravaganza than a fashion show, when the designers of the moment display their creations for the following season. Designers work about six months in advance, so in January and July of each year they show their couture and menswear collections. In October, spring/summer ready-to-wear outfits are shown, while March is the time for autumn/winter designs.

The collections

The collections are attended by fashion buyers and elite members of the fashion press; some celebrity guests may also receive an invitation. On their seats they find a glossy programme or brochure and sometimes a gift. To their guests from the press the hosts will generally send 'freebies' (free gifts) before the show in the hope that they will write a good review of it.

The collections are held in London, Milan, Paris and New York. Although the venue is usually a large arena with a catwalk, more recently some designers have chosen to use less obvious places. The catwalk can be abandoned in favour of stage sets where supermodels put on a cabaret-style production.

fashion's changing face

The fashion of clothing is about the way people dress. Initially people did not wear clothes out of modesty but as a protection against the physical environment. Gradually, as clothes became more sophisticated, a dissatisfaction with the natural body shape (particularly the female shape) developed. Fashions were introduced that altered the appearance, emphasizing and enlarging some parts of the body, and hiding or reducing other parts. This is difficult to understand, especially when you look at some of the tortuous fashions of the past, yet it continues in many societies today.

The desired body shape for any given period is reflected in the way people dress at that time. People have been obsessed with having larger heads, longer necks, smaller feet, broader shoulders or tinier waists. Over the years, explanations for this desire to distort the appearance have ranged from ideas in myths, legends, fairy tales and taboos to political alliances, scientific discoveries, the influence of famous people and media pressure. In addition, **aesthetics** (artistic principles) have played a part, as well as issues of modesty. However, it seems that at no time was any real regard given to the anatomical facts of the human body.

Here, then, is a brief historical snapshot to highlight some of the trends in fashion. It also provides an overview of events in the world of clothing leading up to the present day.

In Roman times, clothing was an indication of social status. ▶

Roman times

During the Roman era, every aspect of daily life was closely regulated, including clothing. For men, there were two basic garments, a tunic and a cloak or toga. The toga displayed a Roman's social status and it was the right of every Roman citizen to wear one. A woman wore a stola underneath a garment called a palla. This was originally like a toga but later covered the entire body and was fastened rather than left loose.

Saxons and Normans

A belted tunic was the standard Saxon garment, worn either long or short. A peasant's tunic was split from hem to waist while a nobleman wore his sewn up at both sides and decorated with a border of embroidery. The female equivalent of a tunic was a gunna and it is from this word that 'gown' originates. It was a simple, ankle-length tunic-robe, often tied at the waist with a strip of matching fabric. The colour depended on the woman's financial status. When out in public a woman wore a coverchief like a scarf over her head and neck.

Late Middle Ages

During the thirteenth century, clothes became more elegant and more practical as a wider variety of fabrics, such as furs and silks, were available from Europe. However, the beginning of the fourteenth century saw a major change in European clothes as the style for men and women began to differ greatly. In contrast to women, men's clothes became shorter and they wore hose on their legs.

The Renaissance

The most significant aspect of these times was the emergence of the middle class, which included merchants and tradespeople. This growing group of affluent people were determined to show off their wealth by imitating the aristocracy. This was clearly reflected in the fashions of the time. Extravagant clothes made of velvet and brocade were deliberately slashed so the silk lining could be pulled through and exposed on the outside.

Other notable fashion items after 1500 included the man's shirt, which developed from the simple linen chemise; the ruff, which was eventually worn by both men and women, and became ridiculously large; and the farthingale, an undergarment worn by women to accentuate the narrowing of their waist.

The eighteenth century

Men continued to wear their coats, waistcoats and breeches but wigs began to dominate the fashion scene. For women, however, fashionable dresses meant exaggerated shapes, whalebone hoops and contorted bodies. Amazingly shaped hats also became 'a must' for fashionable ladies.

The nineteenth century

The French Revolution in 1789 caused fashion to move in the direction of simplicity and comfort for both men and women. Once the **Industrial Revolution** in Britain was in full swing at the beginning of the nineteenth century, textile manufacture became a very important industry. Changes in fashion were by now based on the forms already established in previous centuries: gowns for women and jackets and trousers for men. British tailors became accepted throughout Europe and America and were used almost exclusively for men's clothes. From 1815 the 'Romantic look' was popular and Charles Fredrick Worth emerged as the first **couture** designer in the 1850s. Fashionably dressed Victorian ladies wore crinoline dresses while men wore various styles of coat with fairly tight trousers. Top hats were worn on formal occasions.

twentieth century fashions

At the beginning of the twentieth century lingerie was extremely important particularly the corset. Even young girls were expected to wear one. Corsets were constructed of either cotton or satin insets, gussets and bands. Some were reinforced with whalebone, and a long line of laces down the back ensured a very tight fit. Other items of lingerie, essential for the well-to-do female, included chemises, corset-bodices, camisoles, drawers, petticoats and nightgowns. They were all hand sewn, edged with lace and preferably monogrammed (embroidered with the wearer's initials). It was important that if a lady's skirt was lifted, her black shoes and stockings should contrast with a froth of pure white lace petticoat. Most women did not show their lingerie, of course, but for the musical dancers of the time, such a display was crucial.

Before World War I, well-off men wore striped trousers to work, with morning coats and top hats. For more formal occasions, they wore a frock coat. During the War the fashion market was brought to a virtual standstill, but it was to have a huge impact on fashion styles of the future, particularly for women.

The 20s and 30s

By the 1920s women were gaining independence and a new **emancipated** woman was beginning to emerge. This era was characterized by short bobbed hair, dark eyeliner, flowing dresses and dropped waistlines. Women wanted to look flat-chested and boyish, while the dapper 1920s man wore wide grey flannel trousers known as Oxford bags. The 1930s began with a softer, more feminine outline for women, and the most important accessory of the time was gloves. Gradually, however, the silhouette became more masculine, with square shoulders and uniform-type epaulettes. For both men and women, sports clothes took on greater significance and a casual look was created. Men wore open-necked pullovers, windcheaters and plus fours (baggy breeches, fastened by a band below the knee).

The 40s and 50s

Following the hardship of everyday life during World War II, the fashion industry took some time to recover, but recover it did when in 1947 Christian Dior's famous New Look for women hit the catwalk. The look was very feminine with nipped-in

In the late 1940s, Christian Dior brought his very feminine New Look to the catwalk.

waists and rounded bust and hips. However, it wasn't until the mid-1950s that men's fashion really broke free from the restrictions of the wartime military look. Eventually the Teddy Boy fashion image emerged for men, with slicked-back hair, waisted coats and sharply pointed shoes called winkle-pickers.

Knitwear took on a new role during the 1950s – it changed from being functional to become a fashion item. This was mainly due to the film star Lana Turner, who was known as the 'Sweater Girl' because she wore tight pullovers over a clearly visible stiff-tipped brassière.

The 60s and 70s

Mary Quant is synonymous with fashion in the 1960s. She not only created a new, uninhibited style but opened up boutiques as a new way to market clothes. The so-called 'Swinging Sixties' gave young working and middle-class girls the opportunity to dictate to designers rather than the other way round. They wore mini skirts with clashing colour combinations, and clothes borrowed from men – most notably t-shirts and jeans. As far as the 1960s were concerned, the rules of fashion were there to be broken.

The model Twiggy epitomized the image of the Sixties girl: thin, long-legged, wide-eyed with short baby-doll style dresses. Men wore highly patterned shirts and colourful, tight trousers. Unisex styles began to emerge and were commonplace by the 1970s, especially ethnic costumes, with bright colours, layers, flower prints and puffed sleeves. Influences came from all over the world, including India, Asia, Mexico and the Far East. Jeans and casual wear became increasingly popular. The 'punk' style which characterized the 1970s was thought to be an anti-fashion statement. The young, in particular, wore clothes that were considered to be outrageous and dyed their hair bright colours in an attempt to shock.

The 80s and 90s

By the 1980s, people generally had a better standard of living, with more money to spend. Developments in fibres, fabrics and construction methods meant fashionable clothing was becoming cheaper and more accessible. The introduction of Lycra® gave rise to a fashion of body-hugging clothes, something that would have been totally inappropriate earlier in the century. An increased number of women chose to go out to work so professional-looking clothes such as suits became stylish in the 1980s and 1990s. Men also showed an increasing interest in fashion during this period.

Today fashion designers have less influence over consumers so people are more likely to wear what makes them feel comfortable.

current trends

Technology and fashion

In a discussion about fashion in the twenty-first century, it is impossible not to mention the influence of technology on textiles. Some of today's most influential fashion designers are choosing to use fabrics that were invented with specific technical qualities in mind. Fabrics previously restricted to motorcycling or industrial use are now being used in sports and fashion garments. The unpleasant image of **synthetics** has now been surpassed by a new era of techno fabrics.

The New York-based fashion designer, Donna Karan, has a team of textile designers working on new fabrics all the time. She often uses these as a starting point for her collections, which include shimmering metallics and reflective, high-performance textiles, as well as unusual mixtures such as Lycra® and cashmere.

Synthetic fabrics that were originally developed for demanding sports such as skiing, snow-boarding, surfing, roller-blading, sailing and mountaineering can now be seen on the fashion catwalk. An example of this is Neoprene (a synthetic rubber), which was mainly used for wetsuits but has since been combined with fabrics such as silk chiffon to create a completely new look for clothes.

In the 1960s, French fashion designer Pierre Cardin saw the importance of technology within fabric design when he used vacuum-formed and moulded fabrics. Today a successful fashion designer must accept that the future of fashion lies with fibre technology. Perhaps one day fabrics will be made that not only look beautiful but are able to carry out specific functions, such as releasing vitamins into our skin.

Textile designers

As the emphasis on fibre technology increases in the fashion world, so does the importance of the textile designer. Some fashion designers are starting to employ their own textile designers while others are getting involved in this area themselves. In addition, fashion designers are increasingly relying on computer technology to design and make up their garments. Computer-Aided Design and Computer-Aided Manufacture (CAD/CAM) allow a greater flexibility in fabric design. Pattern repeats can be more varied and knits and weaves can be far more sophisticated.

Shape and style

Of course, the shape and style of clothes worn by supermodels on the catwalk are far more exaggerated and outrageous than most people are likely to wear. Everyday fashions tend to be based on ideas from the collections but are tamed down to appeal to the masses.

These days it is not so easy to state that a particular look or garment is in fashion because British society has become much more accepting of individual style. Fashion is also far more diverse than it used to be, but it is possible to identify general trends. For example, designs are moving towards simple, classic **lines** that show the construction of new fabrics to

Men are becoming more interested and willing to experiment with fashion.

Fashion accessories

Accessories are playing an increasingly important part in today's fashions. Not only does the actual accessory item to be seen with vary from season to season, but what constitutes an accessory is also changing. Body paint, body piercing, body tattoos and hair extensions can now be added to the conventional list of gloves, shoes, scarf, hat and jewellery.

Designer babies

1999 saw the launch of a new range of designer babywear by DKNY (Donna Karan's high-street label), along with other designer baby labels from Guess, Dries Van Noten and Calvin Klein. This perhaps is a reflection of a trend by famous people (such as Victoria Beckham and Madonna) to include their babies in every aspect of their working lives. The clothes are made from itch-free fibres such as linen, silk and merino wool, and the colour schemes include white, pearl grey and black.

their best effect. In addition to the sophistication of manufactured fabrics, though, natural fibres remain in vogue as consumers continue to show their preference for all that is environmentally-friendly.

Women still take centre stage when it comes to interest in fashion design (and fashion designers focus on women). However, men are certainly catching up and taking a greater interest in what they wear. The suit is of course the classic male outfit and seems set to continue dominating the workplace. However, designers are now altering the cut, the fabric and the colour to such an extent that today's outfit seems unconnected with the classic suit. Pale colours are also creeping into the male wardrobe.

Babies of the rich and famous can now be dressed from designer baby labels such as Guess, Dries Van Noten and Calvin Klein.

footwear past and present

In 1955 the British shoe industry employed 110,000 workers and just 9 per cent of its sales came from imported footwear. Today there are around 18,000 people employed in the industry, and imports account for 85 per cent of the sales. Shoe manufacturers in the UK have had to adapt their businesses in order to keep pace with changes in technology and consumer demand. Manufacturers often get their products made overseas while they concentrate on other areas of the business such as brand marketing, design and warehousing. Shoemaking in the UK remains in just a few areas of the country. There has also been a huge cut in the British workforce. In fact, about 75,000 jobs have been lost since the 1960s.

C & J Clark

Clarks shoes are the UK's second biggest privately owned company, yet they have suffered over the years due to the drastic changes that have occurred in the shoe industry. During the mid-Victorian times the village of Street in Somerset was a **tanning centre** for the manufacture of sheepskin rugs and shoes. As the **Industrial Revolution** spread, so shoe making developed from a **cottage industry** to factory mass production. By the 1850s, a third of the population of Street worked for Clarks.

In 1996 Clarks appointed a new chief executive to sort out the company which was no longer keeping pace with changes in the shoe industry. The company realized that the business must be driven by the consumers, so they had to start looking at their customers' needs and wants. This meant a radical shake-up and a large number of job losses. Clarks' UK factories dwindled from twenty down to just four. Clarks also looked at ways of marketing their revamped business. They started to advertise on television and had their shops refitted to give them a brighter, younger feel.

▼ *UK shoe manufacturers often get their products made overseas while they concentrate on brand marketing, design and warehousing.*

Jones the Bootmaker

Jones the Bootmaker was founded in 1857. It began by selling shoes to order that had been handcrafted by the shoemaker at the back of the shop in Bayswater, London. Today there are about 100 Jones the Bootmaker shops around the country. The company aims to incorporate craft, classic style and lasting good taste into all their footwear.

Today at Jones each pair of shoes passes through about 160 separate processes from the careful selection and cutting of leather to the final polishing and packing. There are three main stages of shoemaking:

- *Clicking*
  The clicker matches every pair of shoes through careful cutting of the leather. Clicking describes the sound of the cutter's knife on the brass-bound pattern.
- *Closing*
  In the closing room, skilled machinists sew together the leather uppers and linings. It is here that the shoe begins to take on a three-dimensional shape.
- *Lasting*
  This process involves stretching the upper material over the last (foot-shaped block) and securing it to the bottom of the insole. The shape is retained when the last is removed.

▲ *Boots to get you noticed! These Union Jack platform boots are hardly practical but make a real fashion statement.*

Boots

Boots are stomping their way down all the best catwalks and, just like clothes, footwear has become much more relaxed about what is trendy. There is no longer an acceptable length for wearing boots – they may be worn at the ankle, mid-calf or knee, although thigh boots are less likely to be seen. For men, boots may not appear in different lengths but there are still plenty to choose from. It no longer matters what type of boot you wear, as long as you wear them.

Flat or pointed

Low-heeled or flat boots are usually chosen for their comfort; but while they are practical, they can also look luxurious in leather or suede. Stiletto-heeled boots may not provide the same comfort, but when they are made from material with a brightly coloured snakeskin print they certainly get you noticed! Animal prints are not restricted to fashionable clothes – for example, the leopard-skin effect also applies to fashionable feet.

13

fashion drawing

F ashion drawing, like all design work, is about communication. Sketches are used to convey ideas for outfits and accessories. They may be rough and superficial, just enough to give the feel of a garment. Or they may include precise details of stitching, embellishment, texture – even the cut of the cloth.

Getting started

Sketching of any kind usually requires practice, although certain techniques can help to develop the art of drawing. Some techniques are particularly relevant to fashion drawing. Communicating ideas about clothes can be difficult because people are notoriously difficult to sketch. Of course, garments do not have to be presented on people, but it does help to give a realistic picture of the way clothes will hang when they are worn. All fashion courses are likely to include training in drawing skills.

Drawing people

Most fashion drawings are highly stylized. People are often given a posed stance and drawn out of proportion. However, designers usually learn to draw people in proportion and then develop their own style later. To help draw a human figure in proportion, the body is divided up according to the size of the head. Usually, the total height of an adult is eight times the length of the head. This is a ratio of 8:1. This ratio changes when it comes to drawing children, whose heads are bigger in relation to their bodies. Also, young children are a different shape from adults as they don't develop a waistline until their early teens.

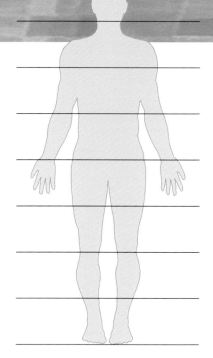

▲ The total height of an adult is usually eight times the length of the head.

Drawing clothes

Fashion drawings should look appealing and reflect the nature of the clothes they represent. The designer must be able to capture the texture of the fabric or the way the fabric falls. Certain graphic techniques known as rendering are used to make clothes look more realistic. For example, by adding patches of white a fabric can be made to look shiny, or by drawing tiny lines, vertically and horizontally, the weave of a fabric is made to stand out.

Fashion drawings are generally shown in three dimensions (3-D), enabling the **client** or consumer to get an overall picture of the outfit or accessory. It is essential, too, that clothes are shown from the back, as the details of this view may be very different. This also applies to accessories such as bags and hats.

Freehand sketches

Different types of drawing are likely to be required at different stages of the fashion design process. Designers usually do freehand sketches to record their initial ideas. These may be in pencil, fineline marker, charcoal or ball pen – in fact any medium that can convey the first impressions of an idea. Often these sketches are kept in a sketchbook containing cartridge paper. Designers keep all their sketches, even the initial rough ones, because they may spark off further ideas in the future.

After the designer has formed their initial ideas, they gradually work on these to ensure they meet the requirements of the design brief. As the ideas develop, the sketching becomes more detailed, showing the design and fabric more clearly. Fashion designers often use layout paper because it allows you to overlay and trace designs as you redraw or develop them.

Working drawings

In fashion, the designer must produce a working drawing that provides the pattern maker with sufficient information to make the pattern pieces. Pattern makers use their knowledge and skills to interpret the details provided by the designer, so the details must be as comprehensive as possible. Often swatches (small samples) of fabric and samples of fasteners are attached to a working drawing to help the pattern maker visualize the whole design.

Presentation drawings

A high standard of presentation is crucial in fashion drawing. Final presentation drawings are often used to present ideas to a client so they must communicate the designs clearly and accurately. The use of colour is important here, as a person's understanding of a design can be greatly affected by the choice of colour or colour scheme. Designers sometimes use markers that correspond with a particular colour reference system called Pantone. Pantone colours correspond exactly to the inks and dyes used to colour fabric.

Fashion designers often use **theme boards** as a starting point for their design ideas, and these may be presented to a client along with the final presentation drawings.

▼ Designers often create a theme board and use it to develop their designs.

designing clothes

A particular fashion or style may look highly attractive to one person, yet ugly or unacceptable to someone else. The reasons for this are likely to be complex, so designing clothes that will appeal to a large number of people requires a great deal of research and skill.

Aesthetics

Aesthetics is all about the attractiveness of something and this cannot simply be regarded as the way something looks. Aesthetics involves a combination of factors that are **inextricably** linked. A particular outfit may be pleasing because of the:

• colour
• shape or style
• way it has been manufactured
• texture of the fabric
• finish or decoration.

To judge whether or not something is aesthetically pleasing, a person must use more than just their eyes. Even before wearing a garment, they are likely to assess the texture of the fabric by touching it.

Designing lines

When designing an outfit, the designer has to consider its **line**. By altering the line the same person can be made to look shorter, taller, thinner or broader. The line does not just refer to the pattern of a fabric; it also means the shape and cut of the clothes. Fabric texture can also have a bearing on the outfit's line. To appreciate the effect of line, consider the following designs:

• A long straight skirt made with a fine pinstripe fabric. Vertical lines have the effect of adding height and making someone look slimmer, because the eye automatically goes up and down the lines.
• A stretch top with thick stripes going across the width. Horizontal lines have the effect of making someone look broader or wider, as the eye focuses on the width, especially if the stripes are thick.
• A shirt in a soft fabric with uneven cuffs and hem. Curved lines will soften any look whether it is in clothes or furnishings. By using a floaty fabric the softened look can be enhanced.
• Flared trousers with diagonal stripes going down each leg. Diagonal lines add to the movement of the fabric and so are particularly effective where a lot of fabric is used.

Designers have to consider the desired outcome from the start, designing the right shape, pattern and texture for the outfit. A good understanding of how clothes are made is important too. They must also choose colours carefully.

▼ *The line of an outfit — both the pattern on the fabric and the cut and shape of a garment — can make a difference to a person's appearance.*

Colourful effects

Of course, a trendy outfit must have a trendy colour, but this does not mean the choice is always easy. Different colours can give an outfit, and therefore a person, a different image or look. Combinations of colour must be chosen carefully to avoid unintentional clashes. Certain colours are associated with particular visual effects. For example, white can enhance someone's size while black can be used to slim down a figure.

In proportion

Usually textiles, whether they are used for clothes or household items, are designed to be in proportion. Proportion is the relationship between the height, width and depth of something. It ensures items look balanced. For example, a wedding dress with a very full and long train would look out of balance if the skirt of the dress was very short. Of course, this may be exactly the look the designer wants to create. An understanding of proportion is important so a designer can appreciate how to achieve a desired effect, whether or not it has a conventional feel.

Proportion or balance is more significant in the design of some items than others. Hats, for instance, need to look in proportion with a person and with their outfit. A large hat may swamp a petite or slight person, while a small pillbox hat may look comical on someone with a large mane of hair and a very full outfit.

▲ Designing clothes requires an understanding of balance or proportion. The length of a jacket or size of a hat can alter the whole balance of an outfit.

The opposite of proportion is disproportion, and many fashions have used this as a feature. In the past, men have worn disproportionately large wigs while women have had to endure tiny waists when compared to the size of their skirts. Contemporary fashion tends to be much more practical for the majority of people, although the late 1990s trend for very high platform shoes could be regarded as creating a disproportionate shape for women.

the influence of Chanel

Chanel has been one of the most influential designers of all time. Her style was always chic and elegant, despite using men's garments as the basis for many of her early designs. At the start of the twentieth century she produced clothes that gave women freedom of movement without losing a feminine look and feel. She began her business at a time when the industry was dominated by men but, because of her hard work, determination and skill, she became a world famous designer.

Coco

Gabrielle Chanel was born in France in 1883. As a child she was called Coco by her father, and the nickname stuck when she sang and danced in the Moulins cabaret as a young woman. She used to sing a song about a dog named Coco and the soldiers in the audience called out the name to her.

Coco Chanel had a tough childhood; her mother died when she was twelve and her father abandoned her and her sisters in an orphanage. However, it was the experience of childhood poverty that drove Chanel to work hard throughout her life. She believed that men gained their power from their financial independence and this is what she wanted for herself. In many ways she was a very forward-thinking woman.

It may have been the idea of wanting to better herself that made Chanel accept an offer from a cavalry officer to leave the Moulins cabaret and become his *coquette* (mistress). It enabled Chanel to live in luxury.

Coco Chanel: one of the first top women designers.

Chanel's hats

As a young woman Chanel was not a classic beauty. Compared with buxom women of the time she was flat-chested, with a small frame – almost tom-boyish. Not to be outdone, she turned this to her advantage by wearing outfits that would stand out or even cause a stir. Unlike the ostentatious hats of the time, Chanel created her own hats with small brims and just a touch of blossom as decoration.

Chanel's style attracted attention from other *coquettes*, and some asked if she would prepare hats for them. Two of these women were famous and photographs of them on stage, wearing Chanel's hats, appeared in the press. In 1910 Chanel's photograph was also published. This was to be the beginning of her fashion career.

Boy

In 1912, Chanel met and fell in love with Arthur Capel, otherwise known as Boy. He was a very successful British businessman, and although he was never to marry Chanel, he did take her as his *coquette*. Boy had a great influence on Chanel's career. He could see her future lay in the fashion business and so, with his financial and business help, she opened a little fashion shop in Paris where she sold her hats.

Sporty style

As she did with all her men friends, Chanel would borrow Boy's clothes, and so she developed a style very much her own. On one occasion she borrowed a sweater to keep out the cold but instead of pulling it over her head, she cut the jumper down the front. She finished off the raw edges with ribbon and added a collar and bow. As soon as she wore it she had instant requests from other women. Many of the clothes Chanel borrowed from men were sporting clothes. As there were no sports fashions suitable for women at the time, she began to design clothes for like-minded sporty females.

Chanel did not sketch her designs or even use patterns. Instead she worked directly with fabric, cutting and pinning it on her models. No one dared say a word while *Mademoiselle* manipulated the cloth, snipping and pulling it to the exact position.

Couture

Chanel's success was such that she soon opened another store. Despite World War I she kept her shops open, and her practical and comfortable clothes were a big hit with women at the time. In 1915 she opened another branch, but this time it was a **couture house** for the rich and famous. Chanel was no longer just popular in France – her reputation was spreading further afield.

Although Chanel did not marry, she had many male companions throughout her life, including the Duke of Westminster. To her, work and independence were extremely important.

When Coco Chanel died in 1971 at the age of eighty-eight, she left behind a legacy of classic styles. Some of her hallmarks include jersey fabric, of which she was very fond and which she used regularly, the tweed (Chanel) suit, the Little Black Dress and the perfume, Chanel No. 5. As she once said: 'Fashion changes, style remains'.

A typical Chanel outfit. ▶

French fashion

Traditionally, Paris has been regarded as the centre of the fashion world. It is the home of **haute couture** and the birthplace of many famous designers. Yves Saint Laurent is one such designer. He is thought by many to be one of the most important influences on French fashion during the twentieth century. However, perhaps his greatest predecessor was the designer Paul Poiret.

Paul Poiret

Paul Poiret was born in Paris in 1879 and died in 1944. During his time as a designer he had a hand in many innovations in the fields of fashion, fashion illustration, theatre, textiles, interior design and fashion photography.

Poiret began his career as an umbrella maker's apprentice but his ambition lay with fashion. In 1899 he joined the couturier Douchet and began to make a name for himself with his first design, a red cape. In 1901 Poiret moved to the **house** of Worth and by 1903 he was ready to open his own couture house.

Poiret was famed for his move away from fashions of the time, which gave women a rigid, idealized figure. His designs freed women by creating a more relaxed shape with fewer undergarments. He is known in particular for the oriental influence in his designs. In the early 1900s, for example, he promoted the **kimono** shape and he later featured turbans in his collections. He also used vibrantly coloured fabrics of orange, green, red and purple, and embellished them with silver or gold embroidery, beading and fur trimming.

Brochures and tours

In 1908 Poiret published a brochure of his designs. They were illustrated by an artist and popularity was such that he commissioned another brochure in 1911. These drawings were later to be superceded by photographs. In 1912 Poiret visited the European capitals with a group of models – the first tour of its kind for a couturier. The following year he made a tour of the United States.

Interiors

After Poiret's first tour he returned to Paris to launch his latest innovation: an interior design school and shop. It was named Martine after one of his daughters, and included a wide range of crafts: glass, ceramics, fabrics, wallpaper, curtains, cushions, carpets and furniture.

With the outbreak of World War I, Poiret closed his businesses and joined the French army. He continued to work after the war but was not able to regain his former status. His designs were now too exotic for the straightforward post-war fashions, so the way was open for new talent.

Paul Poiret's outfits often included elaborate trimming.

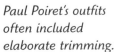

A contemporary design by couture designer Yves Saint Laurent.

YSL

Yves Saint Laurent was not born in France but in Algeria, North Africa. At that time Algeria was a French colony and many families there were of French origin. Saint Laurent studied in Paris and, after winning first prize for his design of a cocktail dress, he was hired by Christian Dior. After Dior's death in 1957, Yves Saint Laurent became head designer at the Dior couture house.

Yves Saint Laurent's style was rather more controversial than Dior's. In 1958 he designed a dress with a 'little girl' look: short, flared skirt, narrow shoulders and semi-fitted bodice. By 1960 he was designing black leather jackets and turtle-neck sweaters. He redesigned modern street fashion for couture rather than the other way around.

Couture house

Yves Saint Laurent's designing career was interrupted when he was called to serve for France in the Algerian war. On returning to Paris, after being discharged on the grounds of ill health, he discovered Marc Bohan had taken over as head designer at Dior. This was a turning point for Yves Saint Laurent. He decided to set up his own couture house and, in 1961, along with business partner Pierre Bergé, the Yves Saint Laurent house was opened.

Ready-to-wear

Following his success as a couture designer, in 1966 Yves Saint Laurent opened a string of ready-to-wear boutiques called Rive Gauche. In 1969 he opened the first Rive Gauche Pour Hommes for the male market. He also launched a range of perfumes for men and women, starting in 1964 with 'Y' and including Rive Gauche, Pour Hommes, Opium, Kouros, Paris and Champagne.

Despite the innocence of his famous peasant look of 1976 (long full skirts, bodices and boots worn with shawls or scarves), Yves Saint Laurent often aimed to shock. In 1992 his winter collection included a dress of faille (rib weave silk) and black velvet with an area of light organza used to expose the breasts.

significant designs

Vivienne Westwood

Vivienne Westwood has her own successful fashion company and has won two British Designer of the Year awards. She also has an OBE. Not only is she one of Britain's most influential designers, she is one of the most outrageous and controversial. She has been criticized for designing clothes that are unwearable and for creating restrictive female garments when women have fought for so long for their freedom.

The punk era

Vivienne Westwood met Malcolm McLaren when she was teaching in the 1960s. Together they opened up a shop in the King's Road in London. By the 1970s Malcolm McLaren was managing a punk group called the Sex Pistols and Vivienne was providing the clothes for both the group and their followers. Her designs involved lots of chains, safety pins, studs and buckles as well as fabrics such as leather and rubber. She provided the punks of that era with a style that would shock. At the same time she gained an enormous amount of publicity for her designs and ideas on style.

During the 1980s Vivienne Westwood outfits took on a completely new shape but they remained just as controversial. She began to set the trend for wearing underwear outside garments, such as a bra worn over a dress. Platform shoes were all the rage but the Westwood version was extreme in both decoration and height – 25cm was not unusual.

These platform shoes illustrate how extreme Vivienne Westwood's controversial designs can be.

Westwood today

Vivienne Westwood may still be regarded by many as eccentric. In addition to her designs, many of her ideas on life are unconventional and are not always acceptable to some people. However, in contrast to most other designers, Vivienne chooses to live in a modest council flat in South London. She travels around the city on her bicycle, wearing her own very showy outfits and when it rains she protects her hair with a plastic bag.

Contemporary Vivienne Westwood collections continue to be extreme and to shock those unused to the designer. Some people say this is just because she has always been ahead of her time.

Calvin Klein

The American designer, Calvin Klein, is probably most closely associated with underwear, in particular men's underwear. Calvin Klein had a theory that male underwear was thought of as a mundane item bought by wives and mothers on the basis of how many

Calvin Klein created jeans with sex appeal by reducing the amount of fabric round the buttock area.

washes it could sustain. In 1982 Calvin Klein was 'road testing' his sample of underwear designs by wearing them to check the fit and durability. By the time the bikini-style briefs were launched, other similar designs were already on the market. However, Calvin Klein's version had one particularly unique feature – his name was incorporated into the waistband. In addition, he spent a great deal of money advertising his underwear as suggestively as the Advertising Standards Authority would allow!

Calvin Klein jeans

Another area of clothing closely associated with Calvin Klein is denim jeans. These were already an essential item of designerwear when Calvin Klein became involved with their production. In 1977 he signed a deal with a manufacturer to produce indigo-dyed, 100 per cent cotton denim, straight-legged jeans. However, Calvin Klein had already done his homework and he knew the look he wanted for his jeans. He had sent out his assistants for several pairs of jeans, including the classic five-button Levis. He then cut each pair apart to see how they were made. To achieve his particular style he had to reduce the area from the waistband to under the groin and pull up the seam running between

the buttocks. This resulted in a look he knew would be popular because it produced a more shapely behind. As with his underwear, he wanted to provide clothes with sex appeal.

The jeans were initially sold at 300 stores already stocking Calvin Klein ready-to-wear collections. He believed that by **mass producing** the jeans, the quality would be improved. Repeatedly making the same garment would ensure that eventually it would be made perfectly.

Designer suits

In Japan a new range of suits for men has recently been launched. The suits feature trousers with pockets adapted to hold mobile telephones while the jacket pockets have been designed to carry compact-disc and mini-disc players. They are aimed at young, fashion-conscious men and are predicted to sell very well.

enduring fashion

Successful designers appear to fall into two categories: those who exhibit a collection that will stun and excite for the moment and those who design with a long-term vision, so that the clothes will endure the test of time. Not surprisingly, many outrageous outfits are never seen beyond the catwalk while other styles become timeless classics.

Christian Dior

Dior's name has long been associated with fashion, perfumes and accessories. His designs have influenced both designers and wearers for many years, and will continue to do so in the future. Dior clothes had an elegance of line that made them more like sculptured structures than fabric garments.

Christian Dior will always be remembered for his famous New Look. The end of World War II coincided with his first **couture** collection in 1947. It gave people the lift they needed after the wartime doldrums. It also gave women the opportunity to be feminine again, if they wanted to.

The New Look

Dior's New Look was defined by very full, calf-length skirts that were pleated, gathered, draped or panelled to emphasize their fullness. Underskirts of tulle (fine mesh fabric) were often used to hold the skirts out. Wide skirts helped to accentuate tiny waistlines and boned bodices added to the overall female look. Dior also introduced hats worn seductively on the side of the head and chokers placed at the neckline.

▲ Dior's outfits allowed women to feel feminine again.

By 1948 Dior developed his New Look for his next collection. Skirts were scooped up at the back and stand-up collars gave outfits a sculptured feel. The 1949 collection was a complete turn-around because skirts became slim, perhaps with a pleat at the back. Many of Dior's designs were to influence future designers, including his three-piece suit: cardigan, simple top and soft skirt. Dior favoured black, navy, blue and white in his collections, and he also used accessories to great effect. Brooches were one of his favourite items, and ropes of pearls wound around the neck – ideas which have been used repeatedly by other designers.

Although Christian Dior's career was relatively short (he showed his final collection in 1957), his excellent reputation was established worldwide.

The Dior **house** continues today producing not only elegant outfits but perfumes, too. Christian Dior always designed for both men and women but he will probably always be associated with the famously feminine New Look.

Jean Muir

London-born Jean Muir is regarded as a designer of classic clothes, and her reputation lives on today in the Jean Muir House of Fashion. Her outfits are thought to have a timeless allure because they are very wearable whilst still exuding elegance.

Jean Muir was born in 1933 to Scottish parents and became involved with textiles at the beginning of her career. She joined Liberty in 1950, working her way from stockroom to sales and eventually sketching in their London store. She broadened her experience further by working for Jaeger from 1956 to 1961. After this she began producing her own clothes, known as Jane & Jane. By 1966 she had set up her own company called Jean Muir.

Jean Muir went from designing ready-to-wear clothes to the high-quality designs of couture. She tended to work with the fabrics she knew best, such as jersey and suede, and she placed great importance on the weight and balance of her outfits. Gradually she developed an international reputation and in 1969 she was even asked by the French to demonstrate the techniques she used to handle jersey fabrics.

Timeless elegance is the hallmark of the Jean Muir Fashion House. ▶

Fashion House

The Jean Muir Fashion House continues to produce timeless, classic outfits that have an easy elegance. The design team place a lot of emphasis on getting the colour, the fabric and the design precisely right for that season. Styles are always subtle and never stiff, and attention to detail is one of the keys to their success.

Issey Miyake

Issey Miyake is a Japanese fashion designer who says he does not like to be 'in fashion'. He is not interested in fashion trends. He wants people to buy clothes because they like them and not because of their label. His aim is for consumers to wear his clothes because they enjoy wearing them and because they wash easily. It is as simple as that.

In 1970 Issey Miyake founded the Miyake Design Studio in Tokyo and held his first fashion show in New York a year later. Some of his early hallmarks include the layered and wrapped look as well as geometric shapes and linear designs. His clothes often show a balance of influences from both the East and West. As a designer, Issey Miyake has long been regarded as a groundbreaker. Even today his design ideas go far beyond those of some of the younger fashion designers.

A-POC

The latest revolutionary idea to emerge from Issey Miyake's studio is A-POC. The name is an abbreviation of 'A Piece of Cloth'. This new concept for clothing of the future was first revealed at a fashion show in Paris in 1998. The idea is about making clothes from a single piece of cloth. This is not revolutionary in itself (a sari is an example of a garment made from one piece of fabric) but Issey's collection was cut and created there and then on the catwalk.

The concept, as revealed at the Paris show, involved laying tubes of flat fabric along the catwalk while a team of assistants cut out skirts, hats, socks, even bags and bras. The items were instantly prepared and ready to be modelled.

DIY A-POC

The new A-POC system of clothing is now available in stores in Tokyo. Consumers choose from a selection of rolls of fabric stored in a display cabinet. Colours include bright red, green, black, navy and white. Sufficient fabric is purchased for the particular item required, along with a set of instructions. Ready-cut A-POC clothes are also available so they can be checked for size.

Issay Miyake introduced a new system of fashion design known as A-POC. ▶

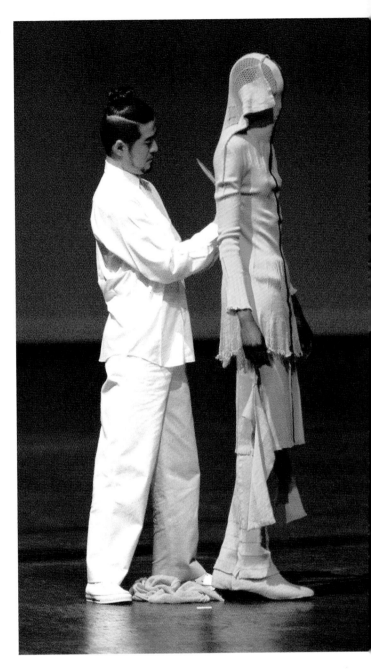

However, another convenient aspect of A-POC is that one size fits everybody and there is no right or wrong way to wear them. Issey Miyake's philosophy is that once you have bought the clothes, you can wear them in any way you choose. In Tokyo, an A-POC outfit costs the equivalent of about £270. In Britain, the price is nearer £480.

Modern technology

However forward-thinking the A-POC system of clothing may sound, Issey Miyake has relied on his creative energies more than his knowledge of modern technology to develop the concept. He now leaves the technological side of designing to textile specialists. They have the expertise to produce new fabrics such as the knitted tubes used in A-POC.

The A-POC system is a completely novel way of manufacturing clothes. Knitting machines are linked up to computers containing extremely advanced software. The result is a knitted tube of fabric which may then have zips and fastenings incorporated during the manufacturing process.

Training for design

After graduating from Tama University in Tokyo, Issey Miyake moved to Paris during the 1960s in order to study design. At the time it was extremely rare in Japan for a man to want to study fashion. In Paris, Issey Miyake trained with the designers Hugo de Givenchy and Guy Laroche, from whom he learnt the basics of **haute couture**. However, while Issey Miyake felt Paris gave him a good training, he did not feel haute couture was the right area of fashion for him. He preferred to design and make clothes for the main bulk of consumers, rather than the wealthy few.

Issey Miyake has been referred to as the 'designer's designer'. He is a highly innovative creator with a very down-to-earth attitude to design.

contemporary fabrics

Despite the many technical advances in fibres and fabrics over recent years, some fabrics will always stand the test of time. However, that is not to say that change does not take place. Denim, for example, has developed over many years; the original workwear fabric has made it onto the fashion scene and it shows no sign of giving up. Denim now has all sorts of end-uses, such as hats, bags, shoes and purses. By combining it with Lycra® it also has the advantages of extra comfort and practicality.

Denim fabric can be updated with a contemporary look by adding beading, appliqué and embroidery. Old jeans can also be cut up and made into a pair of recycled, patchwork jeans – something that has been done by designer Martin Margiela. His jeans sell for around £250.

Natural fabrics

Any fabrics with an environmentally-friendly image are bound to be popular as concerns about human destruction of the environment grow. Natural fabrics such as linen, **hessian** and straw provide the necessary earthy feel to garments. They can be used to make combat trousers, mules, hats, dresses and bags. Canvas and **hemp** have also become popular and are beginning to be used more for clothes and accessories.

Cotton is an obvious choice when it comes to natural fabrics, but you can take it one step further and go for organic cotton as well. Fleece fabric is an excellent choice for jackets, bodywarmers and sweat tops, and now it can be made

by recycling plastic bottles! The environmentally-friendly fleece is produced by breaking recycled plastic into chips which are then **extruded** into a fibre. The fibres are spun to form a polyester **yarn** and knitted into fleece fabric. Another unlikely source for friendly fabrics is recycled tyres, used to produce fashionable shoes and boots.

▼ *Natural fabrics in natural colours are currently popular.*

Check fabrics

Check fabrics are perhaps not everyone's cup of tea, but checks have gradually improved their status. Originally used for school uniforms and tablecloths, gingham is an example of a two-colour cotton check fabric. Today, the classic squares can be seen on shoes, bags and berets as well as on items of clothing. Being a cotton fabric, gingham wears well and provides simple shapes with an unobtrusive pattern.

Sophisticated fabrics

Natural fabrics such as leather and silk continue to add their sleek sophistication to all that's fashionable today. Equally luxurious fibres like cashmere and mohair can be used as either **yarns** or fabrics. To achieve the 'rich' look, tactile fabrics such as velvet, satin and lace are essential, either combined or worn separately. Lace is also widely used, but as a fabric rather than just a trimming.

Technical fabrics

As technology develops, so manufactured fabrics are playing a more prominent role in all areas of fashion. Lycra® is especially important because of its ability to cling to and move with the body. It can even be teamed up with wool and wool blends. Viscose and polyester are being mixed with natural fibres to improve their care properties without affecting the natural look.

French designer Daniel Faret has come up with a shiny, speckled effect for men's suits. The speckles are produced using computer-graph patterns and the wool fabric is **pigment-printed** to give it a rubberized feel. The result is a completely novel fabric and a suit that looks elegant but is also very functional.

Metallic fabrics are also in big demand, and the metallic effect is normally achieved using **synthetic** fabrics, as they can be quilted in such a way that they

Along with natural fibres, bright, bold fabrics are popular today. Shiny and metallic effects are achieved using synthetic fibres.

catch the light. Alternatively, by using a copper wire in the **weft** of the weave, a fabric can be given a soft glow. The copper, coated with polyurethane to prevent it from turning green, can be used to mould the fabric into specific shapes.

Finally, natural and manufactured fibres are brought together to achieve a really unique fabric. Two fabrics are used in the process, one containing 100 per cent black wool and the other a **polyamide monofilament**. They are woven together every two centimetres to create a double fabric with a layered effect. Afterwards the double fabric is dyed blue but the dye is only taken up by the polyamide layer. By heat-pressing the two fabrics, they are brought further together and the hairy texture of the wool traps the smoother manufactured **yarn**. The end result is a blue-black crinkle-look, highly textured fabric.

colour trends

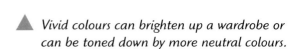

Colour can inspire. Colour can influence. Colour can have a huge impact on our lives. In the area of fashion, colour is crucial. Just as styles are popularized by fashion, so is colour. Natural colours or **hues** are the choice for many fashionable outfits, reflecting society's interest in environmental issues. By complete contrast, clothes can also be bold and bright in vivid or metallic colours.

 *Vivid colours can brighten up a wardrobe or can be toned down by more neutral colours.*

Neutral tones

White is a classic colour for clothes and furnishings; it is associated with all that is pure and clean. Some designers use a lot of white in their collections; from bags to shoes, shirts to pedal-pushers. The use of white is also encouraged by the trend for lace and frills. White clothes naturally require a lot of care but this is rarely a problem with today's easy-care fabrics. However, white can make the body appear larger than it is.

Other neutral hues are also associated with certain fabrics. The deliberate use of natural fabrics such as **hessian**, **hemp**, straw, canvas and linen has encouraged the taste for neutral colours – at least those within the neutral range. Cream, beige, fawn and off-white are all popular choices as a way of giving clothes and furnishings that 'raw' look.

Earthy inspiration

In keeping with the environmental theme, colours are chosen to reflect our natural landscape. Shades of green, brown, orange and red are used separately or together to give fashion an earthy feel. Fabrics that use these tones are also printed with leaf, insect and flower designs to incorporate wildlife into the look.

Bold colours

By complete contrast, the colours of the moment are also brighter and more vivid than ever – whether on a sporty sweat top or sophisticated jacket. Fortunately, vivid colours go well with many of the neutral colours, so they can be toned down if necessary.

Colours that can add a bright spark to anyone's wardrobe include fuchsia pink, custard yellow and lime green. The philosophy behind all these colours is 'anything goes'. Clashing can be OK in fashion.

Futuristic feel

Inevitably the look of the moment reflects the impact of technology on the western world. Not only are highly technical fabrics being used but the colours chosen are providing fashion with a truly futuristic feel. Metallic silver is everywhere: nylon raincoats, bodywarmers, training shoes and body hugging tops. By colouring clothes silver, fashion is creating a space age look which echoes society's desire to get ahead technically. For those who prefer to be more subtle, just a hint of silver or gold can be found on many garments and accessories.

Highly sophisticated fabrics are being used in the manufacture of clothes today and methods of colouring fabric are equally advanced. Fabric can be given the appearance of having a metallic finish or a shimmering shine in the manufacturing process. A graduation of colour can give the illusion that the fabric has simply been dipped in multi-coloured paint rather than dyed.

Finally, although not strictly a colour, fabrics with an opaque finish and transparent fabrics are also big news. So, the new millennium will certainly provide plenty of scope for those who dress to be noticed!

Colours that clash

Traditionally colours that clash have not been used together. For example, 'blue and green should never be seen' is an old-fashioned expression that was supposed to help people remember how to match their clothes.

To find out how colours go together you need to understand the colour wheel. The colour wheel is a way of representing colours. Colours are divided into three types: primary, secondary and tertiary.

1 Primary colours are red, yellow and blue.
2 Secondary colours are orange, green and violet. They are made by mixing two primary colours together. For example, a mix of red and yellow creates orange.
3 Tertiary colours are a mix of primary and secondary colours. So, red (primary) may be mixed with orange (secondary) and so on.

Colours that complement one another are found on opposite sides of the colour wheel, such as red and green.

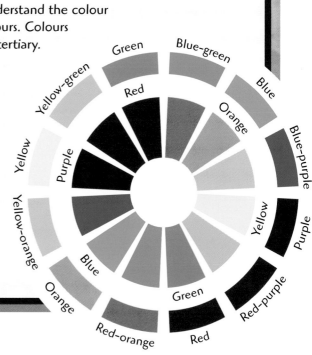

31

studying fashion

Towards the end of the last millennium, many people were fantasizing about designs of the future. This did not just apply to fashion but included ideas about the shape and power of cars, what and how we would eat, even the possibility of holidays in space. When designers start to consider designs for the future they often look towards **predictors**. These are people who spend their time picturing trends and sharing their predictions with the designers.

What follows here are the thoughts from some Year 11 GCSE Textiles Technology students about fashions in the future. They were asked to consider the sort of clothes people would be wearing and the type of fabrics that are likely to be popular during the 21st century.

Rebecca Gambles thinks clothes will be increasingly comfortable and easy to wear. For men there will be sarongs with pants underneath, worn with a long vest top. Children will wear pump-style shoes that fasten like sandals. She also believes that fabrics will interact with the environment, so a pair of trousers may be black when the weather is cold but change to white as the temperature warms up.

Planets play a large role in designs for the future according to Natalie Goodband, who has designed a blue, purple and silver outfit for women. It consists of a long straight skirt which is detachable above the knee so it can also be worn short. Zips feature strongly with one zip travelling down from knee to hemline and another used to fasten a pocket at the front of the skirt. A simple planet design is printed at the bottom edge while the matching top has planets and stars printed all over the bodice. The arms can also be detached using zips and the fabric is smooth and shiny.

According to Fozia Ali, disposable clothes are going to be important. She thinks tops will be made from gold- and silver-coloured paper, and skirts will be long and straight with large frills around the bottom edge. Adam Danning's predictions include men wearing chicken-wire tops and jeans that have zips up to the knee with bows at the top of the zip. Their shirts will be knee-length and worn outside trousers, which may have one leg longer than the other. Unisex clothing will become even more commonplace. For young clubbers, there will be special lasered tattoos that glow under the ultra-violent (UV) lights. Adam also feels the shopping trolley is going to become a very trendy accessory item!

Jamie Cuthbertson's design is for teenage eveningwear. He has suggested very cool, lightweight fabrics due to the heat in nightclubs. His outfit for females consists of a bra-type top with adjustable straps and a floaty layer attached underneath but leaving the tummy exposed. It is worn with a short wrap-over skirt that has a very slight slit on the left-hand side. Clothes that make life more comfortable are seen in Sagina Alyas's designs for the future. She can see tops with built-in CD players, and boots that have wheels like roller skates. In the

Rawzana Akbar's design for fashions of the future. ▶

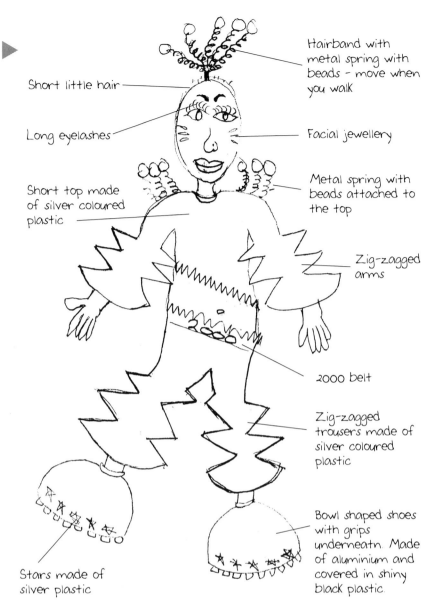

Short little hair

Long eyelashes

Short top made of silver coloured plastic

Hairband with metal spring with beads - move when you walk

Facial jewellery

Metal spring with beads attached to the top

Zig-zagged arms

2000 belt

Zig-zagged trousers made of silver coloured plastic

Bowl shaped shoes with grips underneath. Made of aluminium and covered in shiny black plastic.

Stars made of silver plastic

summer, people will wear large hats for protection against the sun, and their tops will supply cooling drinks of water via a pipe around the neckline.

For Amy Boardman pedal-pushers will take on a new look in years to come. They will be worn with a skirt that has underwiring so that it stands out. She believes metallic colours will be everywhere including blues, greens, pinks, gold and silver. Along with Uzma Jahan, Amy thinks tiny mirrors will feature a lot on clothes and accessories.

What will dictate the fashion of the future?

This is what Jill Sinclair, a GCSE Textiles Technology pupil at Oakwood School, South Yorkshire, thinks:

'*The environment* – scientists predict that global warming will make temperatures soar, so perhaps the fabrics in the 21st century will be specially designed to keep us cool. The hole in the ozone layer allows more harmful ultra-violet rays to reach the earth. New fabrics could be designed to protect the skin from the sun.

'*Our lifestyle* – life has become increasingly hectic for workers and many are trying to look fashionable while juggling a career and family. So, who has time for housework? Disposable clothes made from new fabrics could be a way forward – wear once then throw away and buy a new one. Already fabrics are being made from paper and used to make disposable theatre gowns. Old clothes could also be recycled to make new ones, in the same way as paper is reused.'

fashionable careers

There are a wide variety of jobs and career opportunities within the fashion industry. A small selection is outlined here. Although many companies today provide on-the-job training, there are also various different courses and qualifications to help secure the job you want.

▲ There are many jobs and career opportunities available in the fashion industry.

Creative occupations

Anyone who is interested in design may wish to pursue a fashion design course. This will give them the necessary training to design clothes for a particular company, or on a freelance basis. Working freelance means you are not employed by one company but work on various projects for different companies. Fashion design requires a great deal of creative flare and imagination.

A textile designer produces designs for fabric so creativity is also important. They work with colour and shape and often create their designs using computers.

Scientific occupations

Those with a science background may be interested in becoming a fibre technologist or a textile technologist. This work includes the development of new fibres and **yarns** as well as the improvement of existing fibres and fabrics. A textile colourist will also have a science background but will have specialized in dyes and colour.

Manufacturing occupations

Within the fashion industry there are numerous jobs involving the manufacture of garments. These include machinists, pattern cutters, graders, **layplanners** and pressers. In addition, there are managerial posts such as production manager and warehouse manager.

Journalistic occupations

Many people enjoy communicating through writing, and the fashion industry provides several career options in this area. After gaining qualifications in journalism and fashion, it is possible to become a fashion journalist for newspapers and magazines. In the case of newspapers, this may involve writing features on accessories, hair, beauty and footwear, as well as clothes. However, magazines such as *Vogue* are specifically about fashion, so they have a greater demand for fashion journalism.

Getting qualified

There are many different courses connected with fashion and a whole array of different qualifications. You can attend on a full- or part-time basis and it may even be possible to take some as evening classes. Very specific, short courses are often provided by local colleges of further education. Such courses include tailoring techniques, fashion drawing, bridal accessories, pattern cutting, dressmaking and fashion merchandising.

Degree courses

Degree courses have become more and more specialized so they can give students a more comprehensive knowledge of their chosen career area. Examples of fashion-related degree courses on offer in the UK are shown in the box below.

Other courses that may be of interest to fashion students include:
- HND Footwear fashion and technology (e.g. Stafford College)
- HND Fashion design with CAD (e.g. Northbrook College)
- HND Fashion (sportswear and streetwear) (e.g. Salford College)
- HND Design (textiles design) (e.g. Newcastle College)
- DipHE Fashion, design and clothing technology (e.g. Bradford & Ilkley College)
- BA Design technology for the fashion industry (options in Accessories, Menswear and Womenswear) (e.g. London Institute of Fashion)
- BA Design: costume for the screen and stage (Bournemouth and Poole College)
- BSc Clothing engineering and management – with industrial experience or with a modern language (e.g. UMIST, Manchester)

Course title	Bachelor of Arts degrees (BA)
Fashion	e.g. Manchester Met.
Fashion promotion	e.g. Central Lancashire
Textiles and fashion design	e.g. Ulster
Fashion knitwear design	e.g. De Montfort
Fashion studies	e.g. Derby
Fashion: design with marketing	e.g. East London
Fashion and textiles	e.g. Wales: Newport
European fashion	e.g. Kent Institute, Rochester
Fashion management	e.g. London Institute of Fashion
Fashion and clothing	e.g. Leeds College
Textile design	e.g. Scottish College of Textiles

Degrees and short courses have become more and more specialized allowing the student to pursue whatever aspect of fashion they want. ▶

accessories

The easiest and often cheapest way to transform an image is to add accessories. Some of the latest in these fashionable extras are outlined below.

The scarf

The knitted scarf – a surprisingly simple look from the seventies – frequently returns as a fashion item. Scarves are a great fashion accessory because they come in a great variety of lengths, colours and materials. They can be knitted very easily, using **plain** or **garter stitch** and oddments of wool, with or without the addition of tassels. The chances of a homemade scarf looking like anyone else's are very slim, and it isn't often you get the chance to follow a fashion trend and be individual!

As an accessory, a scarf can change the look of what you wear. It can be used to brighten up an old outfit or it can alter the image of daytime clothes when there isn't time to change before going out in the evening.

Fashion designers interpret the term 'scarf' in numerous ways. They use both woven and knitted fabrics, and these can range from thick and chunky to sleek and shimmery. Designers also vary the way scarves are worn. Some are thrown loosely across the shoulders; others are firmly secured with a brooch. A scarf may be purely for the head or the shoulders, or a combination of the two. It may serve a purpose such as to keep out the cold, or it may have purely **aesthetic** appeal. Scarves don't follow any set rules in fashion, and perhaps that is how they have stood the test of time.

The bag

Like scarves, bags are still predominantly a female accessory, and many women would find it impossible to go out without one. Bags can be divided into several categories – such as handbag, evening bag, school bag, shopping bag – depending on what they are needed for. Whatever the type, bags are very big business. For example, the designer label Gucci makes 61 per cent of its profit from leather goods (where bags are an important item), compared with only 11 per cent on clothes.

In the past, a woman might have carried a small drawstring purse containing a handkerchief or two, but as women's lives have changed, so have bags, in both style and function. Today's handbag may need to hold a mobile phone, laptop and pair of trainers, as well as the more usual items like house keys and cosmetics. The variety of bags now on offer reflects these varied needs. Bags of the moment include those with animal prints, embroidery, beading and lots of colour, though not all at the same time. Like scarves, they express a person's individuality.

The bangle

The current trend for an ethnic look can be achieved very easily by wearing lots and lots of bangles. They are often inexpensive, and come in a range of colours including multi-coloured varieties. Many people like the sound they make as well as the way they look, as they fall against each other along the forearm.

▲ *Bangles can look (and sound!) attractive.*

Styles include plaited leather bands, coloured plastic beads stuck on to leather or plastic, and leather shapes threaded on to a leather strip. Those who want totally original friendship bands can easily make them at home.

The sandal

Sandals are not just a summer accessory – they are fashion items too. Flip flops (comfortable, open-toed sandals) come with their own designer labels and are available in silk fabrics. Sometimes they are also embellished with sequins, beads and tassels, to add a degree of glamour to their practical nature.

Armcuffs are also popular. They are typically made of leather or plastic, and are fastened around the upper arm with a buckle or press stud. The image created by an armcuff depends on how it is decorated. The skull and crossbone or metal studs naturally project a tough image, while coloured beads give a softer look.

Mules are also very fashionable – whether they are the down-to-earth, flat variety that can be worn by anyone, or the evenings-only version with kitten heels and lots of allure.

The friendship band is another way to brighten up arms and legs without spending a fortune. They are worn around the wrist or ankle and come in a variety of colours and widths.

Sandals come in a range of styles and colours. ▶

textile project: backpack

Like jeans, the backpack originally had a very practical function, but both have managed to permeate our everyday lives. The backpack was used by the army and by hikers and travellers, but today it is worn in the high street, in schools and colleges, at work and on the catwalk. In 1985 Miuccia Prada designed a backpack made of industrial-weight nylon and it was to become popular with everyone, regardless of class or culture. The backpack really is the bag to be seen with.

Backpacker's fashion

Clearly the term 'backpack' has been taken from people who travel around the world with their belongings on their back. It is not unusual for young people to 'backpack' around the world before settling down to a job or university studies.

Probably without realizing it, back-packers have launched some trends in the fashion world. Not only has the backpack, or rucksack, been popularized but so have practical items such as the Velcro sports sandal, combat or 'cargo' trousers and khaki-coloured clothing. Popular travel routes include Asia, Burma, Vietnam and Cambodia – so it is not surprising that backpackers have also brought home skirts made from sari silks, little satin bags and *kramas* (Cambodian headwraps). All of these fashion items have been reproduced by top fashion designers, although the originals cost a tiny fraction of the designer versions.

Bags of ideas

Backpacks or rucksacks are not only popular, they are also extremely versatile, so they provide plenty of scope for designers. They can have a tough and functional image. They can be elegant but everyday, or eye-catching for the evening. They can be made large or small – in fact miniature versions make particularly useful handbags. The fabric used can be silky and soft or strong and durable. Practical backpacks also incorporate pockets, so fastenings can be functional like Velcro or buckles. Designers can also add embellishment to the design, such as buttons and bows as well as beads, sequins, piping, stitching, embroidery and logos.

Research a backpack

Before starting to design your own backpack you will need to carry out some research. Don't forget to sketch ideas and make notes throughout your research. First, consider what your backpack will be used for. Will it be a

Designers like Jemima Khan are reproducing Asian styles.

bag for daytime or evening? Will it be functional or **aesthetic**, or both? What is it likely to hold? How many pockets will it need? Will it need to be waterproof? How will it be worn?

If possible, carry out some research into backpacks by looking in shops and catalogues. It may be easier to keep your eyes open and look at all the different bags that people carry. You may have limited access to shops and those shops may have a limited range of designs but the people around you will have picked up their bags from all sorts of places; unusual shops or different towns, cities, even countries.

Asian influence is certainly apparent in western fashion, so you could also research this area. Travel brochures are useful (and free!). They often contain inspirational pictures of countries like India, Vietnam, Thailand, Malaysia, Sumatra, Java or Bali. Or perhaps you, or someone you know, has travelled abroad and has photos that may help to stimulate your ideas? All sorts of images can help with your design ideas, not just pictures of bags.

Your research could also take you to fabric shops to see the range of fabrics on offer. There are likely to be many silks and sari-type fabrics available which may inspire you if your backpack is for a special occasion or for use in the evenings. It is

worth looking at the fabrics available in the first stages of the design process. It can be very disappointing to design something with a particular fabric in mind, only to find it is unavailable.

Design and make a backpack
When you have completed your research, produce some rough sketches of various backpack designs. As your ideas develop, they should show more detail and be **annotated** with notes about the construction, size, fabric type, fastenings etc. Your final sketch should include all views.

To make your backpack you will need to translate your final design into a paper pattern by drawing all the sections that will be needed in its construction – first as a model and then in full size. Remember to allow for seams. Follow your notes on construction as you put your backpack together.

Backpacks started as purely functional. Now they are high street fashion items. ▶

interior design

Surprising though it may be, 'design' is a relatively new concept. Anyone working as a 'designer' before the 1950s was known as a commercial or industrial artist, and held a relatively low status. During World War II the British government began to appreciate the importance of design. Posters were used as important **propaganda** tools. Good design was essential so that their message was clearly understood and noticed by everyone.

In 1944 the Council of Industrial Design was created. Its role was to encourage manufacturers to use design as a way of selling products and to educate consumers about the value of good design. As a result, exhibitions were held at the Design Centre in the Haymarket from 1956. Design Centre Award Schemes were launched in 1957.

Swinging 60s

The 1960s will always stand out as being a time when design really took off, and not just in the area of fashion. The British economy had finally recovered from a post-war recession and was enjoying a consumer boom. There was very little unemployment so people had money to spend and a choice of goods to buy. The sense of freedom people felt was reflected not only in the clothes (such as Mary Quant's miniskirt) but in the interiors chosen for their homes. One designer who made a huge impact on interiors was Terence Conran, who established Habitat in 1965. He started out as a freelance designer then formed the Conran Design Group and two small manufacturing companies, Conran Furniture and Conran Fabrics. Habitat was revolutionary because Terence Conran cut out the middleman and sold his products directly to consumers. He thereby saved them (and himself) money. However, it wasn't just cheaper goods that attracted the public to Habitat. It was a bright and colourful place to buy furniture and accessories for the home. Shopping became fun rather than merely practical.

Conspicuous consumption

Habitat was meeting the new consumer desire for products that looked good and functioned well, but were cheap and could be replaced without a feeling of guilt. Previously, the attitude was that furniture must last a lifetime. However, as attitudes changed, products were made to be expendable – using cheap materials and **mass production** methods. Consumers had a much wider choice of cheaper goods so they could shop more often. Spending money on clothes and products in such an extravagant way is often referred to as conspicuous consumption.

Mass media

The 1960s also heralded the start of an explosion of mass media. Advertisements were not only more widespread (radio, television, magazines etc.) but they were more inventive. Clever one-liners and shocking visual images illustrated the importance of the role of the designer in society. Design was beginning to be seen in its broadest sense – as a method of communication using a visual medium.

Technological designing

The rapid technological changes of the early 1980s gave designers the opportunity to radically change the way they worked. Instead of sketching their ideas, they started to use computer software to create images for them. Gradually, programs were written specifically for different areas of design, giving designers greater flexibility. They began to be in demand by all kinds of businesses, from fast food chains to trade unions. Even schools recruited designers to produce logos and uniforms so that they could have a **corporate image**.

Corporate images were also being used in retailing. Chain stores like Next, launched in 1982 by George Davis, developed a particular look for their shops. Next went for open shelving and wooden floors, and no matter in which town consumers were shopping, the look was exactly the same.

By the 1990s consumer attitudes were veering towards quality. Technological advances meant value for money was becoming a high priority for shoppers. Chairs could no longer be just stylish yet inexpensive; they had to be functional as well. Scandinavian furniture became extremely popular and soon the Swedish company IKEA started expanding into the UK. The company specialized in Scandinavian-designed furniture which was regarded as stylish, well made and inexpensive. In other words, good value for money. Durability had become fashionable once more.

▼ *IKEA has become popular because the Scandinavian-designed home furnishings are stylish and relatively inexpensive.*

41

household trends

Fashion is communicated to consumers through a range of media, and household fashions are no exception. The latest techniques for hanging wallpaper can be viewed on Do-It-Yourself (DIY) television programmes; various magazines are dedicated to showing consumers ways to furnish and fill their rooms; and newspaper articles advocate the latest colours to have in your home. The popularity of BBC's *Changing Rooms* has stimulated so much interest that publishers are also cashing in by producing books on home improvement. Like clothes, household fashion has become big business.

DIY

In the same way that fashion designers are communicating ideas to the public, rather than dictating to them, interior designers are influencing consumers. There is now a trend towards having a go at home interiors rather than leaving it to the professionals. The range of tools, equipment, furnishings and fittings available has also grown tremendously, along with the number of DIY stores. Many shops such as Next and Marks & Spencer have branched out into interiors to meet this growing consumer need.

People are being inspired by ideas seen on the television and in magazines as they realize that they can achieve effective looks for themselves. For example, you can give a room a casual but trendy feel by draping curtains over a pole and gathering them

at one side with a cord or metal tie-back. **Muslin**, **toile** and **voile** are all frequently used for curtains because they allow lots of light through but prevent neighbours seeing inside! These fabrics are now available in a wide range of colours and prices. Other useful techniques for, say, revamping a lampshade or giving furniture a new lease of life can help to transform a home.

Eastern influence

Trends in home design often mirror trends in clothes because there are similar influences on all designers. Styles from the East are popular in the West, and many of these are being reproduced in the home. Although Indian rugs have long been highly prized for their quality and design, other types of Indian furnishings are relatively new to western homes. For example, people buy wooden chests, tables and chairs for their solid appearance and longevity. Carved statues and trinket boxes also provide a taste of India, even if they were bought at the

▼ *Eastern styles are affecting interior design as well as clothing.*

Candles create a soft natural look. ▶

local market. Other furnishings such as cushions, curtains and lampshades can adorn a room with the rich colours and ornate decoration that is characteristic of traditional Indian style. Styles from the Orient are equally popular, with its practical and simple approach to home interiors. Many people have stripped away their **synthetic** carpets in favour of wooden floorboards, covering these with small rugs made from fibres such as **seagrass** or **coir**. You can add more of an oriental feel by scattering cushions of brightly coloured silky fabric on to low-level sofas and beds. Accessories need to be simple to maintain this **minimalist** look, such as a striking flower placed in a neat vase or prints for the wall displaying Chinese or Japanese calligraphy.

Raw edges

Natural materials are an essential part of contemporary interiors. **Hemp**, **jute** and cotton; leather, cowhide and ponyskin; slate, ceramic and wood can all feature in designs for furniture, furnishings, ornaments and practical, everyday items. The look is not just a natural one but raw-edged and rough. Fraying seams can be pleasing to look at and sometimes seams are deliberately made to fray. Raw edges have a rustic appeal and provide a readymade fringe or frill. Wooden items such as coffee tables or book-ends, do not have to be a regular shape and any imperfections in the wood add to its appeal. A rough and ready appearance is what many people prefer.

Animal skins (real or otherwise) are also put to good use in the home. Whether plain or printed, cowhide can be used for

household items such as beanbags, and ponyskin is used to cover cushions and chairs. Instant household items can be made using a selection of hard materials. Slate makes an ideal reminder board for scribbling down notes with chalk. You can stack breeze blocks to create a stand for an ornament or, when topped with a piece of wood, to make an economical side table.

Natural additions

To finish off the natural theme, there is a wide range of home accessories in neutral colours and natural fabrics. For example, candles are very stylish, whether plain, scented, wrapped in bamboo cane or placed on a wrought iron stand.

Ceramics with simple shapes and neutral **hues** need to be carefully placed to avoid making a room look overcrowded. Baskets are also popular, making excellent storage items for stationery, books, magazines, shoes, CDs or just everyday clutter.

resources

Books

The following books are useful for students studying GCSE Design and Technology: Textiles Technology.

Design & Make It! Textiles Technology Alex McArthur, Carolyn Etchells, Tristram Shepard	Stanley Thornes 1997
Examining Textiles Technology Anne Barnett	Heinemann Educational 1997
Textiles and Technology (UK edition) Adapted by Margaret Beith	Cambridge University Press 1997
Textiles Technology Alison Bartle & Bernie O'Connor	Causeway Press 1997

The following books are useful for more detailed information on fashion drawing and design:

Communicating Design (Collins Real World Technology) Mike Finney & Val Charles	Collins Educational 1995
Fashion Design and Product Development Harold Carr & John Pomeroy	Blackwell Science Ltd 1992
Fashion Drawing: The Basic Principles Anne Allen & Julian Seaman	B.T. Batsford Ltd 1993
Introduction to Fashion Design Patrick John Ireland	B.T. Batsford Ltd 1992

I.C.T.

www.firstview.com
Displays recent and current collections from a wide range of designers and provides information about forthcoming fashion shows

www.levistrauss.com
To find out more about Levi jeans

www.textile-toolkit.org.uk
Includes news, competitions, details of events and a chat forum for students. There is also a CD-ROM available for use as a teaching aid for GCSE Textiles

www.worldtextile.com
Provides information about a variety of textile related journals

Places to visit

Luton Museum and Art Gallery
Wardown Park
Luton LU2 7HA
(Tel no: 01582 546722)
*This museum provides comprehensive
information about the hat industry*

The Victoria and Albert Museum
Cromwell Road
South Kensington
London SW7 2RL
(Tel no: 020 7942 2000)
*Textile and fashion exhibitions and Crafts
Council Shop*

Contacts

The Crafts Council
44a Pentonville Road
London NI 9BY
(Tel no: 020 7278 7700)
*Provides up-to-date information about
art and crafts exhibitions and shows; also
produces a magazine called* Crafts,
available on subscription

The British Fashion Council
5 Portland Place
London W1N 3AA
(Tel no: 020 7636 7788)

Journals

World Clothing Manufacturer
Published by –
World Textile Publications Ltd
Perkin House
1 Longlands Street
Bradford
West Yorkshire BD1 2TP
(Tel no: 01274 378800)
Produced for the clothing industry

glossary

aesthetics artistic principles, relating to 'taste'

annotate add written information to a sketch, or label a drawing

client person (or company) for whom work is being done. This could involve designing and making an outfit.

coir tough, rugged fibre used for matting and flooring; made from the outside matting of a coconut shell; comes mainly from India

corporate image the way a company or corporation presents themselves to – or are recognized by – the public; for example, uniforms provide corporate images for airlines

cottage industry a business in which the products are made at home and the output is relatively low compared to the mass production of factories

couture short for haute couture (see below)

emancipated being free from restriction or restraint; often refers to women having independence and their own legal rights

extruded in the production of synthetic fibres, this refers to the forcing of a liquid through tiny holes in a spinneret

garter stitch knitting in which all rows are knitted using plain stitch

haute couture French term meaning high-quality clothes, designed and made for a very limited market

hemp tough fibre, used to make a linen-like fabric

hessian a coarse fabric made from jute fibres

house the fashion industry's term for company

hue another word for colour

Industrial Revolution the period of rapid technical and economic development in Britain between the 18th and 19th centuries; it brought a shift from a farming-based economy to one that was dominated by machinery and manufacturing

inextricably totally involved or bound up with something

jute tough fibre used to make sacks and rope

kimono loose Japanese gown with wide sleeves and tied at the waist with a sash

layplanner someone who arranges the pattern pieces for a garment to ensure the most economic use of fabric

line the visual effect of clothes, affected by the fabric's pattern and texture as well as by the shape and cut of the garment

mass production the manufacture of clothes and textiles items on a large scale

minimalist from the word minimal, meaning 'the least possible', a very simple and understated look; in fashion design this includes simple styles and plain colours; in interior design the look involves a limited amount of furniture and ornaments

muslin very fine, plain-weave cotton fabric

pigment-printed printed with synthetic colourants (dyes); the colourants are not water-soluble so stick to the surface of the fibre

plain stitch type of knitting stitch; used to create plain or garter knitting (see above)

polyamide monofilament nylon formed into single filaments (fibres)

predictors people who are in the business of estimating what products will be available and what consumers will want in the future; may specialize in products or lifestyles

propaganda information distributed often by the government or other political group that helps them in a particular cause; for example, maintaining public support during a war

seagrass hard, almost impermeable fibre which is spun into tough strands that are naturally stain-resistant; mainly grown in China

synthetic made artificially

tanning centre place where leather is made from hide

theme board board covered with pictures, sketches, swatches (samples of material) etc. used to create a mood or feeling about a product to be designed; often used when talking to the target consumer group; also known as a mood board

toile light/mediumweight, transparent cotton-type fabric, used mostly for home furnishings and clothing

voile lightweight, semi-transparent fabric originally made from cotton; it is now also available in silk, viscose or acetate

weft in weaving, the yarns that run the width of the fabric

yarn single strand of fibres that have been spun together

index